Food Service Facilities

Food Service Facilities

SURJEET KUMAR & SANDEEP MALIK

IMSAR, M.D.UNIVERSITY, ROHTAK, (HARYANA)

AMAN PUBLICATIONS

NEW DELHI

Published by
Rajiv Jain for Aman Publications
LG-4A, Ganpati Bhawan,
4675-B/21, Ansari Road,
Darya Ganj, Delhi - 110002
PH: 23255012, 23282127
E-mail: sshjbs@yahoo.com

First Published – 2007
Reprinted-2010

ISBN–81–8204–034-5

SOLE DISTRIBUTOR
JINDAL BOOK SERVICES
LG-4A, Ganpati Bhawan,
4675-B/21, Ansari Road,
Darya Ganj, Delhi - 110002

Jacket Designed by :
S.M. Graphics

Printed by:
NCT Printers , Delhi, India

PREFACE

The food service industry generally encompasses those places, institutions, and companies responsible for any meal eaten away from home. Food service facilities vary from the simplest limited-menu snack bar to the multifaceted hotel food service that may involve public dining rooms, employee dining rooms, cafeterias, banquet service, and room service. Each type of food service facility is characterised by unique traits in the meals offered, type of service, operational methods, marketing approach, customers served, and atmosphere or ambience.

Each food service facility may be planned to meet different objectives. For example, the objective for a fast food facility may stress the speed of service, whereas the hospital food service has to stress the nutritional and therapeutic values of food. These variations indicate the complexity of planning food service facilities. However, there is one characteristic common to all food service facilities. Each is involved in the production and sale or distribution of meals. This common characteristic requires that food service facilities be planned for technologically modern production techniques and operated by modern management concepts.

The food service industry has experienced tremendous growth and change in the last few years, which have created a need for food service facilities capable of providing the variety of meals prepared by different preparation techniques that will satisfy the changing desires of customers. Only those facilities that are planned for flexibility, labour productivity, efficient use of energy, and managed accordingly will survive the competitive environment of the food service industry.

This book provides comprehensive information on current planning techniques, requirements and trends of food service facilities. It will be an invaluable resource for students and professionals of the food service industry.

CONTENTS

1

THE FOOD SERVICE INDUSTRY

The food service industry generally encompasses those places, institutions, and companies responsible for any meal eaten away from home. This industry includes restaurants, school and hospital cafeterias, catering operations, and many other formats. In India the food service sector is right now not much organised as in case of U.S. In some of the major food service providers include: Compass Group, Sodexho, Aramark, and the Crown Group. The companies that supply foodservice operators are called foodservice distributors.

Some companies manufacture products in both consumer and foodservice versions. The consumer version usually comes in individual-sized packages with elaborate label design for retail sale. The foodservice version is packaged in a much larger industrial size and often lacks the colourful label designs of the consumer version.

HOTEL

The *hotel* food and beverage department provides food-related guest services throughout a hotel, conference, or resort property. Outlets for food and beverage services can include the following:

— Full-service restaurant.

— Coffee shop.
— Catering facilities.
— Room service.
— Recreational areas.
— Lobby area bars.
— Food market or delicatessen.

Food items for these combined foodservice areas are provided from a central kitchen, with the exception of large hotel facilities where satellite kitchens provide auxiliary production and service areas. An executive chef supervises production for all areas, consulting with the manager of each foodservice area. Of the seven food service areas, catering affords the possibility for the greatest profit, in addition to providing much-needed cash flow during periods when room sales are slow. Hotel catering services are usually classified as:

— Business.
— Convention/conference.
— Social.

The volume of catering service available to a hotel is based on the size and number of facilities that can be used for private functions as well as the availability of production and service staff and related equipment. The primary catering market for a hotel is based on three factors:

1. Location.
2. Hotel facilities.
3. Customer profile.

1. Location

The location of a hotel determines the demand for in-house catering. In house catering is defined as guest-related foodservice functions associated with business meetings, conferences, conventions, and social concerns. A hotel with a remote location focuses its catering efforts on the business booked into the hotel. Resort locations often provide additional opportunities for catering services at sports facilities and landscape venues throughout the property.

2. Hotel Facilities

A hotel with a suburban or downtown location can expect to develop a large volume of outside catering business, both business-related and social in addition to conferences and conventions. The amount of combined catering business that can be handled at any one time in a hotel is based primarily on the number and size of the facilities available. The major function rooms are usually referred to as the ballroom areas. These are complemented by a series of meeting rooms, some adjacent to the main ballroom area and some located in other areas of the hotel.

3. Customer profile

The customer profile for hotel catering services is made up of both business and social clientele. Customers who use the hotel as a location for a two or three-day meeting consider meal functions as part of the total meeting package. This arrangement not only enables customers to work within a budget that covers the entire project, but also fits with an approach to planning catering functions that considers the success of the overall meeting rather than each individual function.

The catering manager is generally given the responsibility of creating a menu plan for the entire programme along with theme functions and special events. The target market for hotel catering functions is a customer who reflects the social, business, and economic profile of the community. Hotel catering services attract a wide base of customers with a broad range of requests.

Customers who plan business functions on a regular basis are familiar with the catering staff and services of the hotel. Their needs are often quickly identified and provided for. Customers who plan social functions on a one-time basis, however, need more personal guidance throughout much of the planning stage. Pricing is a primary concern of this customer group.

Hotel food and beverage departments are often requested to handle the arrangements for functions to be held away from the hotel property. If a company wants to retain as much revenue as possible from business, convention, and social customers, an off-premise catering policy should be developed. Using the off-premise catering organisational guide, hotel catering departments can easily develop an off-premise catering programme.

Often, a hotel will have the facilities in place to offer a limited menu of take-out items. Items have been selected from the hotel dining room menu to offer to the general public on a take-away basis. Hotels have the advantage over many private catering companies of being able to use their own equipment. In addition, kitchen and storage facilities are available to handle large volumes of both food and beverage as well as equipment. If the volume of on-property business requires the use of hotel equipment, rentals can cover the additional needs, with costs being charged back to the customer.

Restaurants

A ***restaurant*** is an establishment that serves prepared food and beverages to be consumed on the premises. The term covers a multiplicity of venues and a diversity of styles of cuisine. Restaurants are sometimes a feature of a larger complex, typically a hotel, where the dining amenities are provided for the convenience of the residents and, of course, for the hotel to maximise their potential revenue. Such restaurants are often also open to non-residents.

Origin of Restaurants

The term restaurant (from the French restaurer, to restore) first appeared in the 16th century, meaning "a food which restores", and referred specifically to a rich, highly flavoured soup. The modern sense of the word was born around 1765 when a Parisian soup-seller named Boulanger opened his establishment. The first restaurant in the form that became standard (customers sitting down with individual portions at individual tables, selecting food from menus, during fixed opening hours) was the Grand Taverne de Londres, founded in 1782 by a man named Beauvilliers.

Whilst inns and taverns were known from antiquity, these were establishments aimed at travellers, and in general locals would rarely eat there. The restaurant became established in France after the French Revolution broke up catering guilds and forced the aristocracy to flee, leaving a retinue of servants with the skills to cook excellent food; whilst at the same time numerous provincials arrived in Paris with no family to cook for them. Restaurants were the means by which these two could be brought together— and the French tradition of dining out was born. In this period the star chef **Antonin Carême**, often credited with founding classic French cuisine, flourished, becoming known as the "**Cook of Kings and the King of Cooks**."

Restaurants spread rapidly to the **United States**, with the first (Jullien's Restarator) opening in Boston in 1794, and they spread rapidly thereafter. Most however continued on the standard approach of providing a shared meal on the table to which customers would then help themselves, something which encouraged them to eat rather quickly. The modern formal style of dining, where customers are given a plate with the food already arranged on it, is known as Service à la russe, as it is said to have been introduced to France by the Russian Prince Kurakin in the 1810s, from where it spread rapidly to England and beyond.

In India, the restaurants were not very popular till 1940s. Only a few luxury hotels existed in India such as the Great Eastern in Calcutta, Taj in Bombay and Imperial in Delhi.

Some restaurants such as Sher-e-Punjab for Punjabi

food in Bombay, Udupi's for South Indian food were known. In 1947, after partition, many people relocated and started new restaurants in the urban areas, e.g. Tandoori chicken launched in Moti Mahal, Delhi. In 1950s the Modern outlets for middle class got startrd as Ashoka opend in Delhi. The first independent speciality restaurants started in 1960. As the first modern international quality hotel the Oberoi International opend in New Delhi with seven F & B outlets.

Different Types of Restaurants

Restaurants range from unpretentious lunching or dining places catering to people working nearby, with simple food served in simple settings at low prices, to expensive establishments serving refined food and wines in a formal setting. In the former case, customers usually wear casual clothing. In the latter case, depending on culture and local traditions, customers might wear semi-casual, semi-formal, or even in rare cases formal wear. Standardly customers sit at tables, their orders are taken by a waiter, who brings the food when it is ready, and the customers pay the bill before leaving.

In finer restaurants there will be a host or hostess or even a maître d'hôtel to welcome customers and to seat them. Other staff waiting on customers include busboys and sommeliers. Depending on local custom, a tip of varying proportions of the bill (often 10-20%) may be added, which (usually) goes to the staff rather than the restaurant. This gratuity might be added directly to the bill or it may be given voluntarily.

Restaurants often specialise in certain types of food or present a certain unifying, and often entertaining, theme. For example, there are seafood restaurants, vegetarian restaurants or ethnic restaurants. Generally speaking, restaurants selling "local" food are simply called restaurants, while restaurants selling food of foreign origin are called accordingly, for example, a Chinese restaurant and a French restaurant.

Depending on local customs and the establishment, restaurants may or may not serve alcoholic beverages. Restaurants are often prohibited from selling alcohol without a meal by alcohol sale laws; such sale is considered to be activity for bars, which are meant to have more severe restrictions. Some restaurants are licensed to serve alcohol ("fully licensed"), and/or permit customers to "bring your own" alcohol (BYO / BYOB).

Types of Restaurants: Broadly we can categorised restaurants into

1. Full service restaurants
2. Brasserie, bistro, pub
3. Dining car restaurants
4. Fast food restaurants
5. Cafeteria.

Full-service restaurants

Full-service restaurants have the opportunity to offer a variety of catering services to their customers. Before any decision is made to offer these services, however, six important factors should be considered:

— Location
— Customer profile
— Restaurant style or concept
— Staffing capabilities
— Restaurant physical layout
— Cuisine and menu offerings

The proximity of the restaurant to office complexes and centralised business areas will help to establish whether its catering service will be focused on business or social marketing efforts. Businesses in the twenty-first century are spread from urban centres to suburban locations in office parks. Central urban locations offer a concentrated market for both office delivery and take-out. A significant factor in developing the market for business catering is that service is generally required during the business week, leaving weekend periods free to service social business. In addition, locations such as museums, concert halls, and historical sites offer interesting venues to catered functions for both local businesses and conventions.

Both urban and suburban restaurants can successfully develop social catering business. Suburban locations are generally more appropriate for social catering to private homes, clubs, churches, and other facilities. Delivery to urban locations can pose security and logistical problems, creating additional costs for transportation and service labour. Population density also affects the volume of anticipated catering business.

Restaurants situated in rural areas with low population density cannot expect immediate high volumes of catering business. Areas of high-density population yield a variety of catering opportunities that steadily increase in volume through referrals and reputation. The location of the physical restaurant building plays a role in the type of catering services to be offered. Storage facilities, expansion possibilities, and access to major transportation routes are factors important to catering service production.

Restaurants have the advantage of a built-in customer pool to whom they can market in-house and off-premise catering services. In addition, the attraction of being associated with a restaurant's reputation will help to expand the possible market to include new business and social clients. The market profile should classify customers as business or social catering clients, designated by income bracket. In addition the range of activities for which each customer pool will need catering services should be researched as thoroughly as possible.

This will help in developing package programmes along with potential menu programmes and accompanying pricing concepts.

The style, concept, and/or theme of the restaurant should be taken into consideration when planning potential catering services. Off-premise catering services do not necessarily have to blend with the facilities offered by the restaurant. On-premise catering services should, however, be designed to function within the restaurant facilities.

Restaurants facilities are a major factor in providing on-premise catering. The ratio of catering functions to restaurant services that can be handled at a given time is dependent on the size and flexibility of the physical plant. Small private parties are often incorporated into the general dining room setting. Large parties must, however, be given facilities that are separated from the general public. Many restaurants that offer in-house catering schedule large parties, such as weddings, anniversaries, luncheons, and dinners, on days and times when the restaurant is not otherwise open.

Often catering business must be refused because sufficient on-premise facilities are not available. When management is continually turning away catering business, a decision will need to be made as to how the restaurant will balance is future development of catering versus full-service dining services. Kitchen facilities play a major part in determining when and how catering service demands can be met. Kitchen equipment must be flexible, allowing for volume production to take place simultaneously with à la carte restaurant service.

The kitchen cooking load and holding capacity of ovens and auxiliary equipment is important to determine if a kitchen is to be used to its full capacity during busy times. Storage and refrigeration facilities determine the amount of food products available at any given time.

The cost of waste from food spoilage due to lack of refrigeration and freezer space could dilute the profit from additional catering business.

The primary cuisine and menu offerings of a restaurant constitute one of the most important considerations for on-premise catering. Off-premise catering services do not necessarily need to be the same as those offered at the restaurant for full-service dining. Purchasing and production requirements are crucial to the successful development of catering services. On-premise catering should offer menu items that duplicate the established menu as closely as possible in order to enhance production capabilities.

Surrounding items, such as vegetables and starches, are the most effective area of the menu to duplicate. Kitchen production is more efficient when the number of surrounding menu items is limited. Profitable and effective purchasing for catering functions requires that the ingredients for menu items be the same or similar to those on the restaurant menu. This allows the purchasing agent to place orders for maximum volume pricing and quality.

Off-premise catering: The decision to participate in off-premise catering requires a thorough review of a restaurant's resources. A successful in-house catering programme can lead management into perceiving that taking on the challenge of off-premise catering will not cause operational difficulties. Several problems must be anticipated regarding the off-premise facilities in which the final production and service for functions takes place.

During in-house catering functions, service staff can often work between private parties and the dining room, filling in where needed, while the kitchen staff functions as usual, having planned ahead to handle the increased production load. In order to service off-premise functions, however, a separate wait-staff needs to be scheduled. In addition, at least one member of the kitchen production staff will be assigned to the function and therefore will be unavailable to the restaurant kitchen for the time period involved for the off-premise function.

Equipment as well as food will need to be transported both to and from the off-premise function location. Hot food and cold food must be kept at specific temperatures to prevent food spoilage. A refrigerator truck may be necessary at certain times of the year. Transportation routes and problems involving traffic congestion need to be considered in the timing of deliveries. Subcontractors may be necessary for equipment such as tables, chairs, dishes, glassware, linens, dance floors, and tents.

The extent to which a restaurant commits to a full-service catering business determines the amount of extra effort required to handle the increased business. Planning for offpremise catering requires attention to detail. Contingency plans for bad weather, delays in food transportation, and the failure of on-site equipment to function properly should be established in advance so that problems can be dealt with expediently as they arise. Additional costs are incurred when solutions to these situations are not planned for in advance. Contract prices must include these contingencies or management will find that overall costs are higher than the fees charged to the customer for food and services.

Take-out service: Take-out service is the most profitable way for restaurants and catering services to increase revenues without increasing costs. Because take-out service does not require extra seating, it generally will not require an operation to expand its facilities beyond accommodating take-out customers with a pick-up and waiting area. Kitchen production can plan and schedule to handle large increases in volume for short time periods. In addition, take-out does not require the additional expenses incurred by table service for glassware, linens, flowers, menus, and entertainment.

Disposable dishes, plastic flatware, and a carrying container are the basic requirements for take-out service. Successful take-out service does, however, require planning to assure that customers receive menu items in satisfactory condition. As with the catering menu, the selection of take-out menu items should be drawn from the restaurant menu in order to maximise purchasing and production efforts.

Brasserie, bistro, pub

In France, a brasserie is a café doubling as a restaurant and serving single dishes and other meals in a relaxed setting. A bistro is a familiar name for a café serving moderately priced simple meals in an unpretentious setting, especially in Paris; bistros have become increasingly popular with tourists. Mainly in the UK and other countries influenced by British culture, the pub (short for public house) today serves a similar dual menu, offering beer and other alcohol along with basic food fare. Traditionally, pubs were primarily drinking establishments, whereas the modern pub business relies on food as well, to the point where so-called gastropubs are known for their high-quality "pub food".

Dining car

A dining car (British English: restaurant car) or diner (but not "diner car", except in ignorant parlance) is a railroad passenger car that serves meals on a train in the manner of a full-service sit-down restaurant. It is distinct from other types of railroad food-service cars that do not duplicate the full-service sit-down restaurant experience, principally cars of various types in which one purchases food from a walk-up counter to be consumed either within the car or elsewhere in the train. (Grill cars, in which customers sit on stools at a counter and purchase and consume food cooked on a grill behind the counter, are an intermediate type, but on balance could be considered a type of dining car.)

Dining cars have always been prized for the way in which they enhance the familiar restaurant experience by offering a unique form of visual entertainment, namely the ever-changing views of the world outside. While dining cars are less common today than they were in the past, having been not just supplemented but in some cases replaced by other types of food-service cars, they still play a significant role in passenger railroading, especially on medium-distance and long-distance trains. In one of the most common dining car configurations, one end of the car contains a galley (with a side aisle next to it, so that passengers can pass through that end of the car to other cars of the train), and the other end contains table or booth seating on either side of a centre aisle.

Trains with high demand for dining car services have sometimes featured "double-unit dining cars", consisting of two adjacent cars functioning to some extent as a single entity, generally with one car containing a galley plus table or booth seating and the other car containing table or booth seating only. In the dining cars of Amtrak's bilevel Superliner trains, booth seating on either side of a centre aisle occupies almost the entire upper level, while the galley is below; food is sent to the upper level on a dumbwaiter.

Fast food restaurants/Quick service restaurants (QSR)

A fast-food restaurant is a restaurant characterised both by food which is supplied quickly after ordering, and by minimal service. Food purchased may or may not be eaten quickly as well. Often this food is referred to as fast food. In response to increasing backlash against "fast food", the industry has been trying to move the public away from that term over the past five years, shifting to the term quick service restaurant (QSR for short). Consumers still refer to the restaurants as fast-food restaurants despite the industry's efforts to change them. The food in these restaurants is often cooked in bulk in advance and kept hot, or reheated to order.

Many fast-food restaurants are part of restaurant chains or franchise operations, which ship standardised foodstuffs to each restaurant from central locations. There are also simpler fast-food outlets, such as stands or kiosks, which may or may not provide shelter or chairs for customers. Because the capital requirements to start a fast-food restaurant are relatively small, particularly in areas with non-existent or poorly enforced health codes, small individually owned fast-food restaurants are common throughout the world.

Although fast-food restaurants are often seen as a mark of modern technological culture, they are probably as old as cities themselves, with their style varying from culture to culture. Ancient Roman cities had bread-and-olive stands, East Asian cultures feature noodle shops. Flat bread and falafel are characteristic of the Middle East. The modern history of fast food is connected with the history of the hamburger, as the earliest fast-food outlets sold hamburgers as their primary product.

The American company White Castle is generally credited with opening the first fast-food outlet in 1921, selling hamburgers for five cents apiece. White Castle later added five holes to each beef patty to increase its surface area and speed cooking times. White Castle was successful from its inception and spawned numerous competitors.

McDonald's, the largest fast-food chain in the world and the brand most associated with the term "fast food," did not appear until 1948 when a hot dog stand under the McDonald's brand name opened in San Diego. Ray Kroc, the distributor of an industrial milkshake mixer that the original McDonald's used, joined the founders of McDonald's in 1954 and began expanding the franchise. Wendy's, founded in 1972, is credited with pioneering the use of the "drive-thru" window to allow consumers to purchase fast food without having to park or exit their cars.

Fast-food outlets are take-away or take-out providers, often with a "drive-thru" service which allows customers to order and pick up food from their cars; but most also have a seating area in which customers can eat the food on the premises. Finger food comprises most fast food, and can be eaten without cutlery. Fast foods include fish and chips, sandwiches, pitas, hamburgers, fried chicken, french fries, chicken nuggets, tacos, pizza or ice cream, although many fast-food restaurants offer "slower" foods like chili, mashed potatoes, or salads. However, even though Western-style Chinese cuisine is most often served as take-away, it is seldom considered to be fast food.

Preparation of fast food

Fast food is often highly processed and prepared in an industrial fashion, i.e., with standard ingredients and methodical and standardised cooking and production methods. It is usually rapidly served in cartons or bags or in a plastic wrapping, in a fashion which minimises cost.

Consumer spending

In the United States alone, consumers spent about US$110 billion on fast food in 2000. The National Restaurant Association forecasts that quick-service restaurants in the U.S. will reach US$142 Billion in sales in 2006, a 5% increase over 2005. In comparison, the full-service restaurant segment will generate $173 Billion in sales. Fast food has been losing market share to so-called fast casual restaurants, which offer somewhat better and more expensive foods.

McDonald's is a noted fast-food supplier. Opening its first restaurant in 1955, it is a phenomenally successful enterprise, in its financial dominance, brand-name recognition, and worldwide expansion. Ray Kroc, who bought the franchising license from the McDonald brothers, pioneered many concepts utilising standardisation. Implementing strict rules, he introduced uniform products, identical in all respects at each outlet, to increase sales. At the same time, Kroc also insisted on cutting food costs as much as possible, eventually using the McDonald's Corporation's size to force suppliers to conform to this ethos.

International chains

Fast-food restaurants are popular in the United States, the source of most of its innovation. Many major international chains are based in the United States. Consequently, fast-food restaurants have often been the target of globalisation protests, the target of anti-Americanism sentiment and been subjected to attacks because of perceived cultural imperialism. Multinational corporations typically modify their menus to cater to local tastes. However, this practice has not quashed criticism. Additionally, multinational fast-food chains are not the only or even the primary source of fast food in most of the world.

Many regional and local chains have developed around the world to compete with international chains. Most fast food in the developing world is provided by small individual mom and pop eateries. In the developing world, multinational chains are considerably more expensive; they usually are frequented because they are considered chic and somewhat glamorous and because they usually are much cleaner than local eateries.

In the United Kingdom, while fast-food restaurant chains are now common, the British tradition of take-away foods such as fish and chips and steak and kidney pie with mash remain popular. Closer to the end of the 20th century, these have been joined by take-away outlets selling ethnic or pseudo-ethnic foods such as Italian, Chinese, and Indian.

Fast-food chains have come under fire from

consumer groups (such as the Centre for Science in the Public Interest, a longtime fast-food critic) over the past decade. Some of the concerns have led to a Slow Food reaction. This movement seeks to preserve local cuisines and ingredients, and directly opposes laws and habits that favour fast-food choices. Among other things, it strives to educate consumers' palates to prefer what it considers richer, more varied, and more nourishing tastes of fresh local ingredients harvested in season.

Some of the large fast-food chains are beginning to incorporate healthier alternatives in their menu, e.g. salads and fresh fruit. However, some people see these moves as a tokenistic and commercial measure, rather than an appropriate reaction to ethical concerns about the world ecology and people's health. McDonald's has announced that in March of 2006, the chain will include nutritional information on the packaging of all of its products.

Nutritional value

The cooking method used for certain items is partly responsible for those items' higher caloric and saturated fat contents. Deep-fried items fried in shortening or other partially hydrogenated oils (an increasingly less common practice) may absorb trans fats which are damaging to the heart. When served with starchy vegetables such as potatoes (usually deep fried) and sugary soft drink beverages, fast-food meals contain a considerable glycemic load.

Fast-food and consumers

Fast-food outlets have become popular with consumers for several reasons. One is that through economies of scale in purchasing and producing food, these companies can deliver food to consumers at a very low cost. In addition, although some people dislike fast food for its predictability, it can be reassuring to a hungry person in a hurry or far from home.

Because of its convenience, fast food is popular and commercially successful in most modern societies, but it is often criticised for having the following alleged shortcomings, (among others):

— Many popular fast-food menu items are unhealthy, and excessive consumption can lead to obesity.
— Exploitative advertising and marketing are used, especially directed at children (which can have an adverse effect on their eating habits and health.)
— It causes environmental damage through excessive packaging and clearing forests for animal rearing.
— It reduces the diversity of local cuisines.
— Its franchising scheme (royalties).

The fast-food industry is a popular target for critics, from would-be populists like José Bové (whose destruction of a McDonald's in France made him a folk hero to some) to vegetarian activist groups such as PETA.

Cafeteria

A cafeteria is a type of food service location in which there is no table service, whether a restaurant or within an institution such as a large office building or school; a school dining location is also referred to as a canteen. Instead, there are food serving counters/stalls, either in a line or allowing arbitrary walking paths, and customers take food they require as they walk along, placing them on a tray, and pay at the check-out (buffet system). For some food items there may be the system that while at the counter one orders it and it is served by personnel behind the counter. Sometimes, for some food items and drinks, one collects an empty cup, glass, etc., pays at the check-out, then fills that after the check-out. This system may be combined with being allowed to take a free second serving.

Due to the consumption pattern of people, this system is rarely or never used for alcoholic beverages. As cafeterias require few employees, they are often found within a larger institution, catering to the clientele of that institution. For example, schools, colleges and their halls of residence, department stores, museums, and office buildings often have cafeterias. At one time, cafeteria-style restaurants dominated the dining-out culture of the Southern United States, and there were several prominent chains of them: Bickford's, Morrison's, Apple House, K&W, and Blue Boar among them. These institutions, with the exception of K&W, went into a decline in the 1960s with the rise of fast food and were largely finished off in the 1980s by the rise of "casual dining".

However, newer chains, notably Luby's and Piccadilly Cafeteria, have arisen to fill some of the gap left by the decline of the older chains. A cafeteria in a US military installation is known as either a chow hall, a mess hall, or, more correctly, a dining facility, whereas in common British armed forces parlance, it is known as a cookhouse or mess. Some monasteries and boarding schools refer to their cafeteria as a refectory. Students often refer to cafeterias as lunchrooms, though breakfast as well as lunch is often eaten there. Cafeterias serving university dormitories are sometimes called dining halls. A food court is a type of cafeteria found in many shopping malls and airports.

College Cafeteria

A college cafeteria is one that is designed to serve college students at the university. These cafeterias can be a part of a residence hall or in a separate building. Many of these colleges employ their own students to work in the cafeteria. The amount of meals served to students varies from school to school, but is normally around 20 meals per week.

Like normal cafeterias, a person will have a tray to select the food that they want, but instead of paying money, they pay beforehand by purchasing a meal plan. The method of payment for college cafeterias is commonly in the form of a meal plan, whereby the patron pays a certain amount at the start of the semester and the details of the plan are stored on a computer system.

Student ID cards are then used to access the meal plan. A meal plan is not necessary to eat at a college cafeteria however. Meal plans can vary widely in their details to best fit the needs of the students. Typically, the college tracks the student's usage of their plan by counting either the number of pre-defined meal servings, points, dollars, or number of buffet dinners. The plan may give the student a certain number of any of the above per week or semester and they may or may not roll over to the next week or semester. Many schools offer several different options for using their meal plans.

The main cafeteria is usually where most of the meal plan is used but smaller cafeterias, cafés, restaurants, bars, or even fast food chains located on campus may accept meal plans. College cafeterias are prone to having poor food due to the lack of competition. A college cafeteria system often has a virtual monopoly on the students due to an isolated location or a requirement that residence contracts include a full meal plan.

Catering Services

Catering is the business of providing food service at a remote site. Catering is covered by two different groups. Independent caterers and companies with a catering business on the side.

Event Catering

An event caterer serves food with wait staff at dining tables or sets up a self-serve buffet. The food may be prepared on site or shipped in but often some combination depending on the menu and facilities at the site. The event caterer staff is responsible not only for preparing the food but also setting up the dining area and waiting tables. This service is typically provided at banquets, conventions, and weddings. Any event where all the attenders are provided with food and drinks or sometimes only hors d'oeuvres is often called a catered event.

A catering company or specialist is expected to know not just food preperation, but how to make it attractive. A wedding requires working with the entire theme or colour scheme of the wedding. Much catering is sold on a per-person basis, where adding additional people is a flat price per person. Keeping the cost of the food and supplies below this is required to make a profit on the catering.

Mobile Catering

Mobile catering is the business of selling prepared food from some sort of vehicle. It is a feature of urban culture in many countries.

Types of Vehicles

Street cart

A food cart is an motorless trailer that can be hauled (by automobile, bicycle, or hand) to the point of sale, often a public sidewalk or park. Carts typically have an onboard heating or refrigeration system to keep the food ready for consumption. Foods and beverages often served from carts include

— Hot dogs and other sausages.

— Ice cream and other frozen treats.

— Coffee.

Catering truck

A catering truck enables a vendor to sell a larger volume than a cart and to reach a larger market. The service is similar; the truck carries a stock of prepared foods that customers can buy. Ice cream vans are a familiar example of a catering truck in the United States and United Kingdom.

Mobile kitchen

A mobile kitchen is a modified van with a built-in grill, deep fryer, or other cooking equipment. It offers more flexibility in the menu since the vendor can prepare food to order. A vendor can choose to park the van in one place, as with a cart, or to broaden the business's reach by driving the van to several customer locations. Examples of mobile kitchens include taco trucks on the west coast of the United States, especially Southern California, and fish and chips vans in the United Kingdom.

Concession trailer

A concession trailer has preparation equipment like a mobile kitchen, but it cannot move on its own. As such it is suited for events lasting several days, such as funfairs.

Non-commercial Uses

In addition to being operated as private businesses, mobile catering vehicles are also used after natural disasters to feed people in areas with damaged infrastructure. The Salvation Army has several mobile kitchens that it uses for this purpose.

Industrial Catering

Industrial catering includes providing food for airline passengers, schools, prisons and other institutional settings. It can include contract management of client foodservice facilities.

Airline Catering

Airlines often have divisions or hire third parties to provide food for passengers. Food on airlines has dropped in frequency of flights it's offered on. Today a drink and snack item are common on shorter flights. Airline food is often seen as bad by the people who eat it.

Catering Halls

A catering hall is a facility dedicated to private parties with an on-site production kitchen and staff. These facilities can offer a wide range of both in-house and off-premise catering services. Catering halls offer customers a self-contained private function space independent of a hotel or restaurant. Many catering halls specialise in social functions such as weddings and plan the design of the landscaping and building to accent such functions.

This design is also often aimed at a particular segment of the customer market, depending on location of the hall and the density and ethnic background of the surrounding population. Catering halls can also specialise in large functions, providing space for groups that cannot normally be accommodated in other facilities. Such halls are generally designed to host a wide range of social and business functions and a variety of special event themes.

The flexibility, and often the originality, of function spaces are important to the success of a catering hall. Customers will travel considerable distances to social functions held in facilities that offer a unique setting or experience. Wedding receptions are often planned in locations over an hour away from the site of the ceremony so that the bride and groom can have a specific setting for their reception. Catering halls can provide the setting for special event themes ranging from futuristic to country western, offering menu and entertainment packages to match.

The customer target market for catering halls, like hotels, is based on the social, business, and economic profile of the community. Catering halls, also like hotels, are available in a variety of price venues, generally appealing to customers who are looking for menu and function packages within a specific range of prices. Identifying a customer group toward which to target marketing efforts includes surveying the competition, establishing a price range, and determining specific geographic areas of the community in which potential customers live based on demographic information such as annual income, family size, and age.

Catering halls have a great deal of flexibility regarding the type of business that they can solicit. The amount of off-premise catering that can be handled by an operation is limited only by the ability to service it. Location, transportation routes, and population density play a major role in determining this segment of the business. The ability to transport food and equipment and provide service and production staff are other limiting factors.

Role of Independent Caterers

Independent caterers are private businesses offering catering services to the general public. These businesses operate with or without permanent facilities of their own in which to hold functions. Those caterers who operate without a formal facility must arrange for kitchen production and storage space. Kitchen space can be rented from schools, churches, senior citizen centres, and other institutional facilities with commercial refrigeration and production space.

Storage space can be arranged for in self-storage warehouse rental facilities that combine short-term leases with flexible storage space and 24-hour access. Some catering companies have their own production facilities and enough warehouse space to handle large volumes of business. Chairs, floor covering, tables, and the table setup necessary for large functions are either sourced from a catering company's own warehouse or contracted through a local rental supplier. Many independent caterers focus on off-premise catering, maintaining only a small catering hall with limited facilities to house their production and storage needs.

Their focus is on both business and social functions within a wide geographical area. In order to successfully cater to as many functions as possible simultaneously, a catering company has to be extremely well organised. Although equipment needs, staffing, and transportation are major concerns, the primary product, food, is the most important issue.

Private Clubs

Private clubs offer a self-contained facility that operates both full-service dining rooms and private function space along with a variety of food and beverage outlets. Private clubs are generally dependent on their membership for both dining room and catering business. Functioning as nonprofit organisations, clubs are, in many areas, prohibited by law from accepting or soliciting business from nonmembers. If such is the case private clubs may, however, cater functions that are sponsored by members and attended by nonmembers, allowing them to service both social and business activities.

Factors that influence the success of restaurant and hotel catering services, such as location, facilities, and customer profile, also affect private clubs. Off-premise catering services can also be offered to private club members. Private clubs may also contract out their foodservice operation to a contract foodservice operator.

Clubs are broken down into two general classifications: private clubs and country clubs. Private clubs are generally situated in the downtown areas of larger towns and cities. The club facility is used primarily as a location for meetings, private dining, social and business functions.

Country clubs require a suburban location and usually promote a combination of golf, tennis, and/ or boating as their primary recreational facilities. Private dining and catering facilities are located in the clubhouse. Acceptability of location is based primarily on general location and accessibility to major transportation routes. Downtown city locations can create problems regarding parking and security for people travelling into the city.

— *Facilities*: Club facilities can greatly influence the volume of catering business. Clubs offering spectacular settings, access to garden areas for outdoor functions, or well designed interiors will easily attract social business.

— *Off-premise catering*: A club's ability to accept off-premise catering function business is controlled by the same laws and regulations as the solicitation of nonmember business. Beyond these restrictions, the same considerations for restaurants and hotels concerning transportation, staffing, production, and service apply.

Contract Feeding Companies

Contract feeding companies provide institutions such as hospitals and schools, as well as businesses, with in-house meal programmes designed to meet specific needs. Food production and service is contracted for long-term periods with designated budget restrictions. The contract feeding segment of the foodservice industry has been steadily growing since the late 1980s. Major corporations such as Marriott International created large contract feeding companies to service a wide range of customers.

In the late 1990s a separate company, Host Marriott, was created and now operates independently of Marriott International, serving institutional customers internationally. As food costs have increased and available labour decreased, institutions and businesses have turned to outside contractors to operate their foodservice programmes. In most cases, these programmes function as a service to either patients, clients, or employees; they are subsidised benefits, not profit making operations.

By using a professional contract foodservice operator to handle this area of operations, businesses find that the quality of service increases significantly along with client and employee satisfaction. The major factors that can influence the success of catering services within a contract feeding location are:

— *Facilities*: Contract feeding can be offered in a wide variety of dining room and catering facilities. The type and number of facilities that can be used for function spaces within a business or institutional setting will help to determine the volume of in-house catering. Catering functions in these settings are usually business related, but open area spaces can be used by private groups for social functions.

— *Customer profile*: Identifying the customer profile for large and diverse groups of people in a business situation is initially done by job classification level. Private dining room service and business meeting menu selections should be based on the expectations associated with the job levels of the people who attend these functions. The types of food products that will be popular in a cafeteria area depend on the profile of the employee population group. The proximity of the business to an urban centre and the general education level of the customer group, along with local and regional food preferences and subsidy budgets, determine the range of food products offered.

— *Off-Premise catering*: Contract feeding companies working for a business or institution are often called upon to produce foodservice functions in off-premise locations.

Charcuteries and Delicatessens

Charcuteries are food stores that offer take-out foodservice along with gourmet food products. Many of these products are used as ingredients in the preparation of the food line. In some cases a small seating area will be offered for eat-in customers. The trend for home-replacement food is significant to this type of operation. When customers want something beyond fast food for a take-home meal, they turn to establishments that can provide meals that they would like to have prepared for themselves.

Home-replacement food is being provided in a number of types of foodservice facilities, including upscale supermarkets. This type of foodservice operation usually specialises in a regional or national cuisine. Menu items range from salads and sandwiches to fully prepared meals. The success of a charcuterie depends on two major factors: location and customer profile.

Charcuteries should be located where the customer profile supports the level of cuisine offered. Pricing for this type of foodservice operation is generally higher than that of delicatessens and supermarket preprepared and packaged food items; hence it requires a customer base willing to pay for gourmet food products. Smaller independent caterers often operate out of this type of retail outlet, using the facility for both production and storage in addition to a means of advertising and promotion.

Delicatessens are food stores that provide a variety of food products and offer both eat-in and take-out food service. The location should be reasonably close to the targeted customer base. Menu item offerings range from sandwiches, salads, and pizza to preprepared meals-to-go. Take-out foodservice of preprepared foods is a major business segment for this type of foodservice operation.

The profile of customers for a charcuterie/ delicatessen operation is drawn largely from the demographics of the population in the immediate area of the business. Primary customers can be identified as either employees of adjacent businesses or local area residents. A customer profile is determined for each of the two primary customer groups. The local resident profile, with an average check of twelve dollars or more two times a week, may be in the mid-30s to 50s age group, middle to upper income bracket. Further investigation may show that the business employee is a morning coffee and lunch customer while the local resident is an evening customer for home-replacement meals.

Delivery of in-office and at-home preprepared food items can be a profitable extension of a delicatessen's business. From packaged lunches to party trays and platters, delicatessens often provide off-premise food items on a daily basis to a wide range of customers.

2

Food Service Environment

Understanding the Concept of Atmosphere

The concept of atmosphere may be physical aspects such as unusual location, a spectacular view, the method of pouring a drink, or a combination of interior colours, fabrics, spaces and textures, as well as such nonphysical aspects as the attitude of service personnel as exhibited in courtesy, ability, pleasantness, and promptness. The architect, consultants, and designers can develop the physical components of the atmosphere, but it is up to management to provide and maintain its nonphysical components.

Every individual experiences bring some type of reaction to the atmosphere that may be desirable or undesirable. If the individual response to the foodservice facility is favourable, the atmosphere has served to put that person into a good mood. Atmosphere has been identified as one of the inducements for people to dine out. Many people like to be in different surroundings to enjoy the dining experience. In addition to good food and courteous service, the diner is looking for a restaurant that offers luxury or excitement, or at least something pleasant. If customers experience a desirable dining atmosphere, they are more likely to come back because they remember that experience.

Atmosphere is one of the prime generators of repeat business and is an important aspect in the successful planning of foodservice facilities. In the highly competitive commercial restaurant field, the planning of the atmosphere for new facilities is going to be more important. The coming generation of potential customers is growing up in an environment that associates dining out with more than just good food. They will be expecting to experience a variety of feelings, and these feelings will be a direct result of the atmosphere. The planning of atmosphere may well include specialised audiovisual equipment and other electronic devices to help create a particular mood.

Many factors have to be taken into account when planning the atmosphere for a food facility, and they must be considered in light of the clientele who constitute the market. Just as food choice is a matter of individual preference, social custom, income level, needs of time, and so on, the individual's choice of atmosphere is related to many of these same factors. People from varying backgrounds and engaged in different activities will seek out different dining atmospheres. The atmosphere has to be planned to appeal to the particular segment of the market that the foodservice facility wishes to attract. A well-planned restaurant is characterised by both the right menu offerings and the right atmosphere. The most efficiently planned production areas are of little use if there are no customers to serve.

Integration of Marketing

The foodservice industry continues to be more and more competitive, and the integration of marketing concepts into the creation of the atmosphere is desirable from the standpoint of increasing sales. One approach to this integration is to use attractive displays of food and beverages in the dining areas or lobby and lounge areas. Displays of wines, salads, desserts, or baked goods lend to the creation of a pleasing dining atmosphere as well as help increase the sales of these items. The use of salad bars, dessert carts, carving carts, and refrigerated display cases are some of the methods used to accomplish this integration. Among other things, the atmosphere to be developed for a food facility should attract attention, be pleasing to the eyes, and provide an interesting change of pace.

For example, an intimate, peaceful dining room provides welcome relief from noisy offices and industries. Likewise, a noisy cafeteria may actually be refreshing to students who are in quiet surroundings most of the day. The warmth and glow of a fireplace provides a welcome change in cold weather. The development of the physical and psychological aspects of the atmosphere depends in great part upon the planners selected to design the facility.

They must have a clear understanding with the owner of the particular needs and goals to be accomplished in developing the atmosphere. In addition to knowledge of the functional operation of the facility, the planners should be keenly aware of the type of clientele to be attracted. Only then can they come up with a suitable design that will be attractive as well as functional. It is then up to management to develop the nonphysical aspects of the atmosphere to complete the total concept.

Components of Atmosphere

Comfort is one of the key considerations in atmosphere planning. If individuals do not feel comfortable in their surroundings, the atmosphere has not been properly designed. Comfort is created when individuals feel secure and at ease. Security may be psychologically imposed by the use of red and orange colours and by privacy, which can provided by booths and partitions. One way of sing dividers to create private areas in the dining room. Dining rooms which have an expensive look may create feelings of insecurity because individuals feel status-conscious in such surroundings. Atmosphere planning is dependent on an understanding of the perceptual awareness of individuals as sensed through sight, touch, caring, smell, temperature, and movement. The primary considerations of these perceptions as related to a dining experience are summarised as follows.

Sight

The perception of visual space involving lighting levels, colours, eye contact with fixtures and decorator items, and the use of mirrors and screens to expand or contract the visual space.

Touch

Perception of seat comfort, body contact, and contact with floor, tables, tableware, and upholstery fabrics.

Hearing

Perception of noise levels of conversation, kitchen sounds, Aside sounds, and music.

Smell

Perception of cooking aromas, body odors, and material odors from fabrics such as linen and leather.

Temperature

Perception of air temperature, relative humidity, Ay heat, cooking heat, radiant heat, and heat of cooked foods.

Movement

Perception of muscle activity required for access to tables and chairs, movement of servers and other customers, movement outside as viewed through windows. It is important not to think of atmosphere as simply a combination of colours, lights, and spaces, but how the individual is affected by those factors. It is the perceptual concepts that should be kept in mind when developing atmosphere. To clarify the concept of perceptual environment, consider the matter of space. A person's perception of space is measured more in terms of freedom of movement than in terms of physical dimensions of feet and inches. A dining room one hundred feet long means very little to diners. If persons can walk across a smaller room without encountering obstacles, it will be perceptually large.

On the other hand, if they must make their way around closely faced tables and chairs, it will be perceptually smaller. This is due the feeling of crowding when their movements are restricted. Temperature works in much the same way. It is measured in terms of contrast rather than by degrees on a thermometer. An individual .just coming in from the cold will require less heat to perceive a feeling of warmth than someone who has been exposed to a heated room for a long time. The body heat of others is also an interrelated factor is how an individual perceives a crowded condition. Individuals who re in a cooler room may be seated closer together than those who re in a warmer room.

A person's eyes are probably the most important yet deceptive tools of measurement in perceiving feelings. The structure of the eye exaggerates activity or movement that takes place on the periphery of vision. Consequently, individuals can be in an uncrowded room, yet feel as if it is crowded if there is a great deal of action or movement round them. When obstructions are used to block out the activity or movement on the periphery of their vision, they will perceive the area as uncrowded.

Thus, individuals measure the atmosphere with their senses and valuate it as desirable or undesirable. The atmosphere must be tanned so that the individual's perceptions result in a feeling of com-art, ease, and acceptability. With these concepts as a guide, the food facility planner should evaluate the many physical components of atmosphere that can be manipulated and arrive at a combination that ill give the desired sensations. The following are the physical components that affect the perception of atmosphere:

1) Colours
2) Illumination
3) Noise
4) Ambient temperature, relative humidity, odors
5) Type of seating (tables, booths, counters)
6) Furnishings; floor and wall coverings, drapes
7) Table appointments; dishware, silverware, napkins
8) Shape and size of rooms
9) Layout of tables
10) Appearance and dress of employees
11) Menu design
12) Sanitary conditions
13) Exterior design
14) Landscaping
15) Age and dress of customers

Colour

This is one of the visual aspects of the atmosphere as

perceived by individuals; it is also one of the best tools that planners have to create a variety of moods. Most people make a number of choices based on colour; they select their clothes, cars, houses, paints, and even foods by colour. Colour can be used to induce a feeling of happiness, to promote serenity, or to stimulate hunger. It can attract people to one type of dining room and drive them out of others. Certain colours are especially important to the development of dining areas.

Many experiments have shown that certain colours have a very strong emotional effect on most individuals. It is known that blue reduces excitability and therefore helps one to relax. Blue is also considered to be cooling and is "easy" on the eyes. Green is a colour that acts as a sedative. Yellow, on the other hand, is cheery, stimulating, and attention-drawing. On dull, sunless days, people exhibit mental and physical sluggishness which is partially attributed to the absence of yellow, red, and other stimulating colours. Red is associated with excitement and violence. Gray suggests coldness and is very depressing unless it is combined with livelier colours. Colour sensations can sometimes produce physical reactions that are not just of the visual system but affect the entire body. For example, persons exposed to predominately red colours exhibit increased blood pressure, quickened muscular reactions, and greater emotions.

Red also tends to produce restlessness and makes time seem to pass very slowly. In comparison, persons exposed to predominately blue and green colours have been found to exhibit slower muscle response and quicker mental and conversational response. Blues and greens also make time seem to go faster. Some of the common emotional responses caused by exposure to various colours. These may be used to develop the type of response desired in various areas of the food facility. The colours have to be predominant in an area and individuals must be exposed to them for a period of time.

Features of Colour

The strong effect colours may have on individuals, care should be taken in selecting them to achieve the desired result. One if the aspects of good colour planning deals with contrast. A single predominant colour, no matter how pleasing, cannot function alone. A restful green that is predominant would strain the part of the eye susceptible to it and eventually lead to eye and body fatigue. With a single predominant colour individuals would have to look harder to distinguish objects because of the lack of contrast. Extreme contrast between very light and dark colours is also undesirable since they too result in eyestrain. Achieving the right amount of contrast along with maintaining the desired emotional responses is necessary to the creation of a pleasing environment for dining.

Classifications

Red, yellow, and blue are the primary colours. They are referred to is primaries because other colours are derived from them. In their pure form the primary colours are too strong to use on large areas and therefore are used as accents. The secondary colours are green, orange, and violet and are mixtures of two of the primary colours. Green is obtained by mixing blue and fellow, orange by mixing red and yellow, and violet by mixing red and blue. Mixtures of primary colours and secondary colours result in the intermediate colours. Examples of intermediates are red-orange, yellow-green, and blue-violet.

Colours are also classified as warm or cool. Red, orange, and yellow are the warm colours; they seem to advance and convey a feeling of warmth. The cool colours are blue, green, and violet; these are retracting colours and are cooling and relaxing. A combination of one warm colour and one cool colour results in the complementary colours used in colour planning.

The problem of selecting colours that go well together or harmonise is solved by using one of five rules. These rules are related to harmonies and are identified as monochromatic, analogous, complementary, split complementary, and triad. Monochromatic harmony uses a single colour and is the simplest of colour schemes. The single colour can be expressed in the following ways.

— As the pure colour itself

— As a tint of the pure colour (a tint is the pure colour mixed with white) is a shade of the pure colour (a shade is the pure colour mixed with black)

— As a tone of the pure colour (a tone is the pure colour mixed with both black and white).

— Analogous harmony is obtained by using any three or four consecutive colours on the colour wheel. Examples of analogous harmony are red-orange, orange, and yellow-orange; or red, red-orange, orange, and Glow-orange.

— Complementary harmony results by using any two colours that are directly opposite each other on the colour wheel. Red and green, red-orange and blue-green, or yellow and violet are examples of complementary harmony.

— Split complementary or near complementary harmony involves three colours. Any one of the two complementary colours and two colours adjacent to the omitted complementary colour are used. On the colour wheel, the split complementaries are in the form of a Y. Examples of split complementary colours are yellow, blue-violet, and red-violet; green, red-orange, and red-violet; and red, blue-green, and yellow-green.

— Triad harmony also involves three colours. These are selected by king every fourth colour on the colour wheel. Two examples of triads are red, yellow, and blue; and yellow-orange, red-violet, and blue-green.

— After a particular harmony is selected, then a decision regarding the tints, shades, or tones of the colours is made. One or two of the colours selected will be used for the walls and other major surfaces. The other colours will be used as accents on smaller objects like drapes, table cloths, and dinnerware.

The important points in colour selection are as follows:

— Pure colours are usually too strong and brilliant when applied to large areas or surfaces.

— Colours should be selected under the kind of lighting that they will be used under. Colours selected under fluorescent lighting will appear different under incandescent lighting.

— Colours selected from a small sample will appear brighter when applied to large areas.

— Complementary, split complementary, and triad harmonies always result in a combination of warm and cool colours. The desired atmosphere will dictate which colour is to predominate.

— Black, white, brown, and gold usually go well with any of the colour harmonies.

— Texture is closely related to colour application and usage is best considered at the same time the colour choices are made.

Light and Colour

As light modifies colours in many ways, the type of light source and systems of lighting should be considered when selecting colours. Pink lights, for example, have been shown to pale lipstick colours. Green lights have a tendency to show up wrinkles and should not be used in an atmosphere where a feeling of well-being is to be created. Another problem is the use of amber lights which tend to wash out colours. A well-chosen colour scheme can be easily spoiled by poorly selected lights. Lights and colours for work areas are quite different from those desirable for dining areas and should be planned separately.

The uses of colour in foodservice facilities are so numerous that space will not allow a complete presentation of all of them. Therefore, a guide to the uses of colour is presented below. Note that many of the uses of colour are related to other factors that affect an individual's perception of atmosphere.

1) The use of warm reds, browns, yellows, golds, and oranges enhances the appearance of foods.
2) Where emphasis is to be placed on fast service and high turnover, warm colours should dominate the major areas.
3) Use colours in dining areas that are flattering to people. Colours that tend to make people look pale (green and grey) should be avoided.
4) Use light colours in small areas to create the impression of size.
5) Use warm colours in rooms that are windowless.
6) High ceilings can be made to appear lower by using dark colours.
7) Emphasising horizontal lines by dark colours will make a ceiling appear lower.
8) Low ceilings can be overcome by emphasising vertical lines with dark colours.

9) The end walls of long narrow rooms should be a warmer or deeper hue than the other walls to make them approach and make the room seem squarer.
10) Undesirable features of a room can be painted the same colour as their background so as not to emphasise them.
11) Each room or area should have a mixture of warm and cool colours.
12) Adjoining rooms or areas are best painted in harmonious colours.
13) Avoid using too many different colours in one room or area.
14) Use light colours to make objects appear larger if they are to be emphasised.
15) Use dark colours to make rooms appear smaller.
16) Use brilliant colours to bring attention to signs or other features.
17) Dark-coloured objects appear to be smaller than they really are.
18) Maintain proper contrast to permit differentiation of objects from their backgrounds.
(19) Avoid highly reflective colours that tend to tire the eyes.

The selection of colours is a very difficult task that requires skill, taste, and experience. Colour scheming does not end with the blending of wall colours with upholstery, fabrics, and carpets, but includes the considerations of menus, dinnerware, uniforms, and even the type of decorations. Just as the right colours can be used to make a food facility more attractive, the wrong colours can focus attention on features that should not be accented. Also, since colour is so influenced by fashion and trend, these factors must be considered in the colour scheme chosen.

LIGHTING

As with colour, proper planning of lights can achieve dramatic effects and aid in the creation of the desired atmosphere. Both sexes enjoy a type of lighting that makes them look their best. This factor is of great importance in the planning and design of lights for dining areas, bars, rest rooms, and other public spaces. The best system of lighting for restaurants appears to be a combination of indirect, direct, and spot lights. These lights can be arranged to accomplish the desired flexibility required for the various meal periods. Areas should be well lit for breakfast and lunch, while less lighting is desired for evening meals. The installation of rheostats will provide this flexibility. In considering the lighting system, the amount of daylight entering an area should be considered. Total glass area can be specified by the architect to adjust for this factor. The use of tinted glass may be considered for some situations.

The ultimate type of lighting for dining areas has traditionally been considered to be candlelight. The reddish flame of candlelight is flattering to people and to most foods. The flickering of the flame adds to the creation of a desirable atmosphere. Alternatives to candlelight are incandescent and fluorescent lights. The economy of operation of fluorescent lights favours their installation in large areas. Incandescent lights would be the best choice in dining areas because of their red colour enhancement. Properly selected fluorescent lights may also be used in dining areas if sufficient red tones are used in the colour scheme. The deluxe warm white fluorescent tubes are the closest in colour tint to incandescent bulbs and would be recommended.

As with colour, lighting can do much toward creating atmosphere by correcting spacial deficiencies and accenting desirable areas. To illustrate, a low ceiling can be made to appear higher if it is well-lit; high ceilings will appear lower if they are dimly lit. Care should be taken not to light the long walls brightly in a narrow room since it will appear to be even narrower. Dark walls will show up better with bright lights, and if the colour is to be accented, the illumination level has to be high. Bright lights are placed above normal eye levels to minimise glare. The same concept applies to candles since they too can create glare. Candles may be placed in frosted globes if they are at eye level or slightly below.

In dining areas, it is best to concentrate illumination on the seats and tables and perhaps on special design features. The ceilings and walls should not be so brightly lit that they detract attention from the room. Bright lights may be used to create a brisk atmosphere which, if service is fast, results in a high turnover of customers. Serving areas, should be well-lighted. Some operations may use full lighting for a high turnover at lunch and then dim the lights for evening meals in hopes of attaining higher check averages.

Colourful Lights

Careful selection of coloured lights will enhance the total atmosphere. The first consideration is to coordinate the coloured lights with other coloured objects and colour schemes used in the room. This is important, since certain colours will take on strange off-colours when subjected to coloured lights. Red colours will appear very dark under blue or green lights and olive-green colours look brown under yellow lights. Coloured lights affect the appearance of the faces and clothes of people. Red lights have the advantage of flattering complexions and tend to enhance the colour of fabrics. Red lights also have a good effect on most foods.

Green and blue lights are undesirable for illuminating areas where people will be present. These lights tend to distort the red hues and are unflattering because of this. Green and blue lights may be used for inanimate objects that serve as accent pieces. The use of pink, ivory, or amber lights is suggested for areas where skin tone is important, as they are warm and impart a friendly and inviting feeling. It is better to use tints of colours rather than strong hues.

Lighting should not only provide atmosphere but should reach a satisfactory level of illumination from a practical standpoint. If the lighting level is too high, individuals will have a feeling of exposure; or if too dim, they may feel fearful. For these reasons, there should be enough light so persons can see, yet not so much that they feel uneasy. One method of attaining such an arrangement is to lower the height of ceiling fixtures. This provides a sufficient amount of light and at the same time results in a comfortable soft effect.

Foodservice lighting levels typically will range between 5 and 50 foot-candles (53.8-538 lux), with 30-50 foot-candles (323-538 lux) usually used for breakfast and lunch. A level of 5-30 foot-candles (53.8-323 lux), depending on the atmosphere desired, is used for evening meals. The lighting level in all areas must be sufficient to make the other elements of the atmosphere visible. It is senseless to spend a great deal of time and money creating a striking colour scheme and then ruin it with poor lighting. Any area with less than 5 foot-candles (53.8 lux) of illumination may as well be colourless.

In reality, the excitement of good lighting comes largely from its shadows and variations in brightness. Flat, shadowless lighting is dull and monotonous. The general lighting system for an area needs the accents of bright areas which come from direct light sources. These may take the form of wall brackets, chandeliers, downlights, or spot lights. Recessed ceiling downlights of low intensity are very satisfactory for lighting dining areas.

SOUND

Aside from dinner music, sounds are to play a passive role and never attract attention. The design goal is to create a balance between quiet and noise. Many people are uncomfortable in a room which is very quiet. A noisy room creates tension and irritability. For dining rooms, a satisfactory acoustical environment has a reverberant sound level that is high enough to be heard, but not so high that individuals at nearby tables can distinguish what is being said. Correct planning for the acoustical environment contributes to the development of the desired atmosphere. The sensitivities of individuals to various sounds require control of undesirable noise and maintenance of desirable sounds at an acceptable level.

Sound may be considered to be a pressure wave and is compared to the ripples spreading out from a pebble dropped in water. If the sound is not restricted, it will spread out in all directions. The speed of sound in air is about 1100 feet per second (335 meters per second). Any sounds produced in open air will travel directly from the source to the listener. In a room, however, sound is reflected from the walls, floor, and ceiling and can build up a general sound level much greater than that which results from the same source in open space.

Sounds that are repeatedly reflected become noise or unwanted sounds. Noise at a high enough level causes irritation and fatigue. It can interfere with communication and concentration and become very distracting and disturbing. The intensity of sound is measured by the decibel. A sound intensity of one decibel is at the threshold of audibility for the normal human ear. A sound intensity of 20 decibels may be compared to a whisper.

The normal speaking voice has an intensity of about 60 decibels. Any sound intensities over 100 decibels for any length of time are undesirable, and constant exposure can cause partial loss of hearing. When there is a source of sound in a room, the level of noise at any position is made up of two parts. The first part is the direct sound travelling straight from the source to the position under consideration. The second part is the reverberant sound, which is the sound reaching the position after multiple reflection from the room surfaces.

The intensity of direct sound falls off as the distance from the source increases. Direct sound is reduced by about 6 decibels each time the distance from the source is doubled. Reverberant sound levels will generally be at a uniform intensity throughout the room. Direct sounds are predominant at positions close to the source, while reverberant sounds will dominate positions remote from the source.

Problem of Noise Controlling

The problem of controlling noise levels is basically a matter of suppressing the sounds from the source or reducing the amount of reverberant sounds. Sound-absorbing materials are used to minimise both types of sounds. In some instances, the source of the sounds can be isolated by coverings or baffles. Kitchen areas are very difficult to soundproof because of the materials used in the construction of the room and the large amount of metallic equipment present.

Hard, dense materials, like quarry tile or clay tile used for kitchen floors and tiled wall surfaces, reflect a large portion of the sound striking them. Stainless steel surfaces actually act as sound surfaces much like a drum. In these areas, it is desirable to increase the amount of sound-absorbing materials as much as possible to overcome the severe noise problem. Service doors leading to the kitchen can be vestibuled to reduce the noise level before reaching the dining room. This is a compromise between the additional square footage needed for the vestibule and the desirability of reduced noise levels. Thus a facility designed for professionals may include a vestibule while a facility to be designed for other segments of the market may not consider one.

The following things that can be done to minimise noise from the kitchen include the following:

1. Selecting mechanical equipment such as fans and compressors for quiet operation.
2. Using installation techniques that minimise duct noises, the sound of water flow, and water hammer.
3. Using silent closing devices on doors and drawers.
4. Providing rubber bumpers for mobile equipment.
5. Soundproofing walls between kitchen and dining areas.
6. Placing a service station between the entrance to the kitchen and the dining room.
7. Creating a quiet work environment to reduce employee noise.
8. Using the spread load dishwashing concept where an adequate inventory of china, silverware, and glassware are maintained to handle the entire meal period. Dishwashing begins after the meal period to clean the dinnerware for the next meal period. This concept has several ramifications in terms of soiled and clean dish storage requirements, dishwasher size, impact on employee scheduling, and the total size of the dishwashing area.

In addition to acoustical treatment of walls and ceilings, carpeting where permitted will also help. Local sanitarians should be consulted before specifying carpet for production areas. The sound-proofing of metal surfaces by undercoating will reduce the noise created. One method of handling noise problems in dining areas is to vary the spacing of tables. The distance between diners at one table should be appreciably less than the distance to diners at adjoining tables. If a greater density of seating is desired, the use of screens or partial partitions will reduce the sound levels. Bar areas tend to be noisy and can be partially partitioned.

Music

Music is a desirable sound is one way of enhancing the audible environment. Music has a direct effect on the mood of individuals. Background music should be selected so it does not attract attention. It should be soft, inoffensive, and as characterless as possible. The correct use of background music can put customers in a good mood for dining.

Climate

This is one of the important factors affecting the comfort of people. Most individuals are very sensitive to thermodynamic phenomena and variations from an ideal climate are easily noticed and quickly lead to discomfort. Customers will quickly respond to environmental conditions that are too hot, too cold, too drafty, too stuffy, or too damp. The ideal climate for dining consists of temperatures between 70 and 75°F (21.1 and 23.9°C) with a relative humidity of 50%. Thermodynamic comfort is a function of activity and other factors such as age, sex, and the amount of clothing worn. Needless to say, the climate should be designed for the particular type of patron that the facility is to be planned for. Higher-priced operations will usually attract people who are accustomed to slightly higher temperatures.

Women prefer higher temperatures than men, and children require less heat than both men and women. People who are in active occupations prefer lower temperatures. The amount of clothing worn during the different seasons reflects the needs of different temperatures. People will be wearing lighter clothing in the summer; therefore, slightly warmer than normal temperatures would be appreciated. Clothing worn in the winter is heavier and temperatures should not be allowed to get too high. The effects of colours and lighting are evaluated before a particular temperature level is decided upon.

Temperature can be used to some extent to affect a desired turnover of customers. Many fast-food operations may want lower temperatures to keep the customers on the move and thereby increase the turnover rate. The opposite is true in more luxurious dining rooms where turnover is not stressed. Customers are inclined to be more relaxed in a higher temperature, and the warmth is conducive to a leisurely meal of several courses. The ideal design is to have a system where the temperature can be precisely adjusted for the particular situation. Climate control in most regions requires both heating and air conditioning. The systems should have sufficient capacity to maintain the desired temperature and relative humidity.

Pleasant Odors

Climate control also includes the control of odors. Odors are an important part of the atmosphere, because smell usually evokes much deeper memories in individuals than either vision or sound. People are often uncomfortable in odor-free surroundings, and pleasant odors can contribute to the desired atmosphere. The popularity of display cooking areas in the dining room is partially caused by the cooking aromas that are emitted. Odors have to be controlled or they will blend and can become quite offensive. This is very noticeable in dining areas where the air circulation system may bring in varied kitchen odors. Mixing the odors of fish and steak, for example, is not at all appealing to the person eating the steak.

Odors are very disturbing to individuals when dining because taste is largely a matter of smell. If the odors cannot be controlled and separated, or if they are undesirable, they should not be allowed to seep into the dining room. One method of accomplishing this is to maintain the air pressure in the dining room at a higher level than the air pressure in the kitchen. Exhaust systems designed to rid the interiors of smoke, fumes, and odors should be positioned to avoid affecting the immediate exterior environment. This is especially important for exterior walks and entrances into the public areas.

Furnishings

Furnishings for the dining area are also correlated to the type of atmosphere to be planned. The first thing that an individual does upon entering a dining room is to look for a place to sit. Therefore, arrangement of tables, chairs, and auxiliary furnishings does much to affect the initial impression of customers. Many people do not like to sit at exposed tables because they feel observed. This problem is overcome by the use of booths or by planters that act as partitions.

Tables and Chairs

Tables, chairs, and banquettes should be large enough to seat diners comfortably without crowding. Distances between tables are sized to enable waiters or waitresses to move through the area while serving and allow diners to eat and converse without being distracted. Selection of chairs is critical since the greatest body contact is made with them. Chairs must have suitable shape, angle of seat and back, size, relationship to table, and tactile qualities to be comfortable.

Table space of at least 26 in. (660 mm) should be allowed for chairs without arms to provide elbow room. Armchairs require a minimum table space of 28 in. (711 mm) for comfort. The preferred height of chair seats is 17 to 18 in. (432 to 457 mm), for adults. A minimum of 12 in. (305 mm) of space is needed between the top of the chair and the bottom of the table. The shape of the table should be considered in relation to the dining mood to be created. Round tables, for example, tend to promote communications among the diners and may result in a lower turnover but higher check averages. Square or rectangular tables tend to increase turnover and are more efficient in the use of dining space.

Counter seating can be used to accommodate single customers and also increase turnover rates. Combinations of tables, booths, banquettes, and counters are frequently planned to appeal to a variety of market segments. Cashier areas should be placed for ease of access and in consideration of flow patterns. Bars, buffets, wine displays, or other merchandising setups are placed for maximum visibility and exposure to the customers.

Fabrics

The selection of drapes, carpeting, and fabrics is guided by the need for variations in textures, colours, and shapes. These materials may be chosen to blend with or contrast with the architectural features of the building. Drapes and floor coverings are selected to give an overall appearance of unity and balance. Various fabrics are selected to add warmth and cosiness to a room and to relieve any monotony in the shape of the room. Fabrics contribute not only by their visual impact, but by the fact that they are more pleasant to touch than hard surfaces. Designers may use grass wallpapers, ceramic tile, cork, linen, silk, brick, and other materials that are textured and appealing for wall coverings. Carpeting adds a feeling of intimacy and comfort because it is a point of contact.

Pictures and Prints

Pictures and prints used to decorate wall areas add considerably to the atmosphere. An advantage in using these items is that they can be easily changed. The pictures selected should not clash with the decorative scheme. The shape and size are correlated to the walls on which they will be placed. Colours within the pictures or on frames should blend with the overall scheme of the room to give a coordinated appearance.

Table settings can enhance the appeal of the dining atmosphere. Customers notice the tableware they are using and will thus form an impression of the restaurant. Each item placed on the table is selected to add to the feeling and mood to be created in the room. This pertains to dishes, glasses, silver, napkins, and tablecloths.

Food Facilities or Exterior Design

The term exterior, as used in food facilities design, is taken to include signs, landscaping, parking areas, building structure, doors, and windows. The objective of exterior design is to attract customers. To perform this function effectively, the exterior must convey the correct impression of the type of food facility into which the customer is being invited. Exterior design is to be coordinated with interior design to provide the total atmosphere.

Problem of Visibility

One problem to be dealt with in exterior design is the matter of attracting initial attention. This is a problem of visibility as seen through the eyes of pedestrians and people in slow- or fast-moving cars. An attractive sign, large enough for the situation, is generally accepted as the best method of attracting attention. The placement of the sign must ensure that drivers are aware of the facility before it appears in view. In some locations, signs may have to be placed at considerable distances from the building. The most effective signs are those that are short and to the point.

Attraction is also gained by the exterior treatment of the building. This includes the size, shape, colours, and materials used in construction. The first impression of an interior of a facility is gained from the exterior. This impression- is derived not solely by the exterior design but from glimpses of the interior that are provided by windows. Windows are so located as to frame the parts of the interior that they expose.

Colour usage on the exterior can follow the same general guidelines presented for interior use. An additional consideration is to let any natural landscaping provide much of the colour. In this case, the building elements can be finished as plainly as possible so as not to compete.

Floodlighting is frequently used with success when the architectural features of the exterior are appealing or dramatic. Care must be used in sizing and placing windows in floodlighted areas to prevent glare into the building. Some designers may prefer to rely on the elegance of simplicity and use little, if any, decorative detailing. On the other hand, facilities with perhaps a national theme may require carefully selected exterior details to complete the concept of total atmosphere.

Planning of Parking Areas

Parking lots and areas is important in creating the right impression with the customers. The ease of entering and leaving the parking lot as well as the individual parking space is critical to good design. Consideration should also be given to the placement of walkways from the parking lot to the building. The locations of exterior trash and garbage containers have to be selected carefully. It may be desirable to sacrifice a parking space or two to give special treatment to these undesirable areas. The customers' first impression of a foodservice facility as they leave their cars should not be the sights and smells of trash and garbage. Management should stress the cleanliness of exterior areas at all times.

The entrance door to the facility can form the climax of the exterior attractiveness. It should be selected in accord with the overall design of the building exterior. Doors may be all glass, half glass, wood, or metal, plain or with panels. Separate entrances to the bar are provided if the bar will be used by nondiners. Entrance doors are located for easy access from streets or parking areas. Whether to provide an entrance area or not is largely a matter of choice. An entrance area can have several desirable functions: it can convey a sense of spaciousness and enhance the atmosphere. Entrance areas also provide a meeting place for people and can be used is waiting space during rush hours.

Landscaping provides the setting for -he facility. Another use of landscaping is to hide undesirable service areas or views from dining areas that are not pleasant. The landscape architect may use contours, plant textures, heights, rocks, pathway surfaces, or garden furniture to achieve the desired exterior appearance. In laying out the landscape, important views are selected and foregrounds and backgrounds are developed for them. The landscaping must harmonise with the exterior features of the building so that a good impression is created from all angles of view.

EMPLOYEES

The importance of retaining good employees and keeping them in a pleasant mood cannot be underestimated as a vital part of the atmosphere. A cold welcome, poor service, or indifferent attitude can ruin all the friendliness which the colour, lighting, decor, and furnishings have created. These physical components of the atmosphere are ineffective unless they are complemented by the human components.

3

Functional Areas

Introduction to Functional Areas

In the day-to-day operation, all foodservice facilities perform various functions. These functions common to most operations include receiving, storage, preparation, production, service, warewashing, and waste disposal. These functions can easily be related to the materials and products involved in the food facility. Other functions that are performed it are not easily related to materials or products include accounting, purchasing, management, and communications. Typically, each function can be broken down into more specific items.

For example, the general storage function may be subdivided into storage of meats, dry foods, beverages, linens, dishes, silver, supplies, and trash. The functional planning for the various areas of foodservice facilities may be accomplished in different ways. Experienced foodservice consultants have developed their own techniques of planning and can an areas fairly rapidly.

The first step in functional planning is to visualise all the necessary functions to be performed in the proposed foodservice facility. This obviously comes easily to experienced planners, but persons unfamiliar with planning may find it helpful to make a list of the functions.

Each function consists of a number of tasks. For example, the tasks involved in the preparation function may include weighing, cutting, mixing, blending, panning, moving, and judging quality. These tasks vary from one facility to another depending upon the method of operation desired by the owner or manager. The method of performing the tasks also depends on the type and form of materials involved, the kind of equipment to be used, the quality of finished products, and the skill of the persons involved.

The evaluation and selection of these variables that affect the tasks are a part of the designer's responsibility. Hopefully, the best choice of materials, equipment, and processes will be made, to facilitate performance of these tasks. Thus functional planning begins with identification of functions and visualisation of the tasks to be performed for each function.

Physical Requirements

The basic requirements considered are equipment and space. For each function or task, the planner will determine the type of equipment to be used, and this in turn leads to the development of space requirements. The capacity of the equipment is not usually determined at this time because a careful analysis of the menu and scheduling are required. In the development of equipment and space requirements, the planner has to decide how each of the tasks for a particular function is to be performed in terms of the materials and processes involved.

To illustrate, consider the task of making a stew as one of the components of the cooking function. Some of the variations of the materials that may be used in making the stew are:

1. Entirely from fresh raw ingredients; both meat and vegetables

2. Partially fresh vegetables and partially canned (i.e., fresh potatoes and other canned)
3. Partially fresh vegetables and partially frozen vegetables
4. All canned vegetables and fresh meat
5. All frozen vegetables and fresh meat
6. Fully processed canned stew
7. Fully processed frozen stew

It can be seen that each of these variations in the ingredients will require different tasks and different processes for production. This in turn leads to different equipment types. The planner will evaluate the menu items to be produced and make the decisions regarding the type of production equipment to use. This same concept is used for all the other functions and tasks required to operate the facility. Considerations of space requirements are also evaluated in a similar manner. The mere identification of the functions and tasks alerts the planner to the fact that some kind of space will be needed.

The planner does not necessarily need to determine the final square footage of space now, but does consider whether a particular task requires floor space, work space, and/or storage space. The designer is essentially developing the basic concepts for the operation of the facility. This is done prior to the planning of the actual physical areas. In other words, the planning of the operational methods is the key to the functional planning for the facility. A short discussion of some of these functional areas will illustrate and clarify the concept.

Receiving Function

The receiving function is very similar for most: foodservice operations. The receiving of incoming foods, beverages, and supplies is planned according to the types and volumes of different materials handled. The frequency of deliveries and the type of delivery service are considered for each type of material to be received. For large facilities, materials-handling systems may be utilised to simplify the movement of materials into and out of the receiving area. Many suppliers offer their products in palletised form, which simplifies the movement. The use of carts, trucks, and conveyors will solve most materials-handling problems. Planning of the materials-handling system for the receiving area is only a part of the total system for the entire facility, and the planner should consider all the various components of the handling system before making a final decision.

Some may decide to use a single type of handling equipment for everything from the initial receiving to final service. Other planners may conceive a system which uses several types of equipment, each selected for its characteristics for handling certain types of materials. For example, mobile carts and trucks may be selected for handling food items, while conveyors may be chosen to handle dishes and other nonfood items. The availability of a wide variety of materials-handling equipment enables the designer to develop many different systems. Some temporary storage in the way of floor space and table space is required to check deliveries for quantity and quality. This space is designed on the basis of the larger amounts of frequently delivered materials.

Additional space is planned for scales, storage of skids and hand trucks, and for other necessary equipment for the receiving function. Consideration of waste disposal is also a factor in planning for the receiving function, since some partial trimming and cleaning of materials may be needed before they are placed in storage. Disposal of boxes, cartons, and other packaging materials removed during the receiving function is also involved. Architectural features, including the size and location of unloading docks and doors, may be developed at this time.

Storage Function

Planning for the storage function in food facilities includes dry storage, refrigerated storage, freezer storage, beverage storage, and storage for nonfood supplies.

Dry storage: The dry storage function, like other storage functions, is necessary for the on-the-site storage of frequently used materials. Storage requirements will depend upon the types of materials, frequency of delivery and the volume of each delivery. These variables are evaluated before functional planning of the storage area begins. Dry storage areas for food items are planned to maintain temperatures between 50° and 70°F (10° and 21.1° C).

The desired relative humidity is approximately 50%. For this reason, heat-generating equipment, such as motors and compressors, should not be planned for this area. Pipes carrying steam or hot water are insulated to minimise heat gain of the storage area. Protection against moisture from sweating cold water or refrigerant lines is also important. Planning for protection of the foodstuffs from insects and vermin is required for sanitary reasons. Some space for storage of frequently used dry items can be provided in various work areas of the facility. This concept will reduce the amount of movement required to obtain the materials.

Refrigerated storage: Refrigerated storage areas maintaining temperatures of 32°-37° F (0.0°-2.8° C) are required for fresh meats, vegetables and fruits, dairy products, beverages, and carry-over foods. Many planners are specifying smaller but more numerous reach-in refrigerators strategically located throughout the facility instead of one large walk-in storage. The use of reach-in units minimises employee movements in obtaining items. A combination of walk-in and reach-in refrigerators seems to be a good design for many types of foodservice facilities.

The reach-ins are usually located adjacent to preparation and production equipment or may be built-in under tables and counters. The design of walk-in refrigerated areas is similar to the dry storage areas except for the refrigeration system required to maintain the desired temperature. The size and type of foodservice operation and the frequency and volume of deliveries will determine whether a walk-in refrigerated space is needed. It is thought that a walk-in refrigerator is feasible for operations serving over 300-400 meals per day.

Reach-in refrigerators are generally designed to store for a shorter period of time and are ideal for smaller operations. Pass-through refrigeration units may be specified where their use will simplify the storage and movement of foods. The increased use of frozen foods necessitates planning refrigerated space for thawing purposes. Requirements will depend on the volume and type of frozen foods to be used in the operation. Thawing space is generally designed to handle one day's production.

Freezer storage: Temperatures of -10° to -15°F (- 23.3° to - 26.1° C) are needed to safely store frozen foods. Designers are aware of the increased use of frozen foods that are partially or fully preprocessed, and plan accordingly. Some operations have gone almost exclusively to frozen foods. Freezers may be walk-in or reach-in, and requirements are dictated by several factors including the availability of seasonal items. The possibility of buying seasonal items in volume lots should be evaluated before the design of freezer storage is finalised.

Storage of nonfood items: The design of storage areas for nonfood items like dishes, glasses, flatware, utensils, paper goods, linen, cleaning supplies, and furniture can take many different forms. They may be stored in rooms, on shelves, in cabinets, or on specially designed racks. In smaller operations, some items may be incorporated in the dry food storage area, but separate areas are best for larger operations. All chemicals, soaps, sanitising compounds, and other cleaning supplies should be stored separately because of their danger to foods. Separate areas are also desirable for cleaning equipment such as brooms, mops, pails, scrubbers, and polishers. In-process storage of items may be accomplished by special equipment such as self-levelling dispensers. The self-levelling dispensers are a very satisfactory method of providing storage for dishes.

Preparation Functions

The preparation functions for a foodservice facility are meat/fish/ poultry preparation, vegetable preparation, salad preparation, and sandwich preparation. Speciality restaurants may have different or additional functions depending on their menu items. An example is the fish and shellfish preparation function for seafood operations. The various preparation functions are sometimes combined and performed in one area. Smaller facilities frequently combine the salad and sandwich preparation areas. Combined vegetable and salad preparation areas are also common.

Meat/Fish/Poultry Preparation Functions

The meat/fish/poultry preparation function consists of cutting, chopping, grinding, and portioning of these items and their products ready them for further processing. The preparation function has fanged drastically over the years with the advent and increasing use of fully preportioned products. Some operations may have minimal [eat/fish/ poultry preparation areas where the only tasks involved are to opening of packages and the panning of the items. Larger operations and commissary operations may still require a full meat/fish/poultry preparation function. The planning for the meat/fish/poultry preparation function varies with the amount of preparation that will be done on the foodservice pemises.

Function of Vegetable Preparation

The vegetable preparation function historically involved preparing primarily fresh vegetables for cooking and salad production. Typical tasks associated with fresh vegetable preparation are trimming, peeling, washing, cutting, and chopping. As with meat preparation, the vegetable preparation function can be minimised by utilising various types of preprocessed vegetables. Canned arid frozen items are generally used as alternatives to fresh vegetables. Design and planning for the vegetable preparation function depends on the state of the raw materials and the subsequent tasks to be performed. Large operations choosing to use fresh vegetables will require the use of cutters, choppers, slicers, peelers, and similar equipment. Type and capacity will be designed to handle the volume of vegetables to be prepared. Holding refrigerators are used if the preparation is done a day prior to usage. Waste disposal is another aspect in planning for the vegetable preparation function.

Function of Salad Preparation

The function of salad preparation is that of combining and assembling ingredients prepared in the vegetable preparation area, or obtained from fruit and vegetable areas, into finished salads. Various quantities of meat, fish, and dairy products are used in certain salads. The preparation of some appetiser items may also be a part of this functional area.

Design for the salad preparation function will depend upon the type and volume of salads to be produced. Salad and vegetable preparation functions are frequently combined in smaller facilities. Another alternative is to combine the salad preparation with the sandwich preparation function.

Large foodservice operations, especially those serving banquets, will design for a separate mass production salad area. In this situation, assembly line concepts and related equipment can be utilised. The perishibility of salads necessitates planning of refrigerated holding facilities. Mobile refrigerated carts are selected by some designers as a method of transporting and holding the finished salads. Pass-through refrigerators are frequently specified for cafeteria operations.

Functions of Sandwich Preparation

The design of the area for sandwich preparation is based on the need for fast and efficient work methods. The work areas are planned to provide ample space for the ingredients used in the sandwiches, and tools, and a normal flow of work.

Custom-designed sandwich preparation areas are used for operations handling a large volume of sandwiches. In some cases the sandwich preparation area may be in part of the serving area, as in cafeteria or counter-service operations. Assembly-line techniques and automatic wrapping machinery are typical designs found in institutional and in-plant feeding operations.

Cooking Function

The heart of all foodservice facilities is the main cooking function, and special care in planning for it is required. In addition to cooking ill meat and vegetable items, the cooking area serves as the hub between the production and service functions. In many table-service operations, for example, the pick-up of food for serving is directly adjacent to the main cooking area. The design of cooking areas varies from very limited facilities, as in fast-food and limited-menu operations, to the very extensive facilities of luxury table-service operatic or in large institutional food-services. In all cases, the design of cooking area is closely correlated with the various menu items to be processed.

Baking Function

Except in a relatively few cases, foodservice operations will not be involved in the production of a full line of baked goods. Even many large institutional operations in universities and hospitals confine heir baking function to cakes, cookies, and pastries, other items being obtained from commercial bakeries. Even the operations that do a good portion of their own baking will use basic mixes that simplify he tasks of the baking function. Full bakeries are occasionally planned for commissaries or central kitchens that supply several outlets. These may be planned to handle the conventional tasks of formulation, scaling, mixing, handling, and make-up.

The advent of high-quality pre-prepared unbaked goods that require only thawing and baking has also had an impact on the design of baking areas. Many of the pre-prepared items can be processed in the main cooking area, eliminating the need for a separate baking area completely. An economic analysis of the cost of full baking on the premises versus the use of pre-prepared baked goods may also influence the design of the baking system.

Serving Function

The different ways of performing the serving function result in a variety of serving facilities that may be planned. Basic table-service operations require pick-up areas immediately adjacent to the cooking battery. Separate pick-up areas are used for salads, beverages, and desserts. Some items, including rolls, bread, butter, and water, are stored at waiter or waitress stations located in dining areas. Serving-line facilities are planned for cafeterias, employee feeding, and school or university feeding operations. Several- configurations of serving lines can be used, depending on the total number of people to be served and the time allowed for serving.

Straight-line configurations, are the most basic and are characterised by easy access and well-defined traffic flow. The major problem with the straight-line configuration is its limited serving capacity per line. Variations of the straight-line include the U-shaped counter and the herringbone design. These configurations give more linear space and increase serving-line capacity. The sopping centre or scramble serving line system is characterised by an open-square configuration of counters at the perimeters that allow traffic to flow freely in the centre.

Total serving capacity of the shopping centre or scramble system is much greater than that of the basic straightline configurations. Other types of serving functions that may be planned are tray make-up conveyors for hospitals, cart assembly areas for banquets, and room service facilities for hotels. Each of these has special requirements and should be planned for efficient handling of the food to be served.

Dishwashing Function

The dishwashing function is usually performed in a separate room or area that has to be well ventilated and illuminated. Acoustical tile and noise-absorbing materials are used to aid in lowering the high noise levels associated with this function. Modern dishwashing machines can be obtained to handle any volume of dinnerware. Glass washing, which used to be a major problem in food facilities, now better accomplished through the control of washing, rinsing, ad water additives.

In many cases it is possible to wash glasses satisfactorily if they are washed shortly after the water has been changed their operators may prefer to have a separate glass washer. Large hotel foodservice operations find it desirable to provide a separate silver room where silverware can be cleaned and polished the separate silver room provides a better means of control over the expensive silverware. The design of the dishwashing area is dependent upon the total volume of dinnerware to be washed and the time required to accomplish the washing.

Some operations may prefer to carry a large dinnerware inventory in order to spread the washing over a long period of time. This usually occurs between the meal periods. Others may wide to carry a minimum dinnerware inventory and must therefore ash the items as soon as they are soiled so they can be returned to service immediately. Regardless of the system to be used, the designer will provide methods of sorting, soaking, washing, and drying of the various dinnerware items. Appropriate handling and storage methods are also devised for both soiled and cleaned dinnerware.

Pot and Pan Washing Function

The pot- and pan-washing function is also preferably done

in a separate area instead of combining it with other areas as some small operations may be inclined to do. The basic pot- and pan-washing function can be handled with a three-compartment sink and sufficient space for storing the soiled utensils. In some operations, a large storage area for soiled utensils may be required because they are not washed as soon as they are received. This occurs when the same personnel who wash dishes also wash the pots and pans. Pot-washing machines are considered for large food facilities if they can be economically justified.

Waste Disposal Function

Every foodservice operation has different requirements for waste disposal and many factors should be evaluated before designing a system to handle this function: amount of waste generated, type of waste paper, plastic, garbage, cans, etc.), cost of hauling and dumping, frequency of pickups, and stricter air and water pollution laws. Some of the waste disposal systems that may be used are described as follows.

— *Compaction*: The use of compactors is usually considered where large volumes of disposables are to be handled. Compactors quickly reduce the volume of waste so that it can easily be handled in smaller nits. The weight of the compacted waste should preferably be less than 50 lb. (22.7 kg) for convenience in handling.

— *Incineration*: Incinerators can be used to some advantage if the cost of equipment needed to comply with local codes is not prohibitive. Pollution ordinances should be checked for requirements.

— *Grinding*: Garbage grinding is generally allowed in areas with municipal sewerage systems. However, some communities may not allow garbage grinding if they experience problems with nonbiodegradable materials such as completely plastic or plastic coated materials.

— *Pulping*: Waste pulping creates a liquified waste by using heavy-duty rotary grinders with a recirculating water system. The liquified waste is then processed through a water extractor where it is reduced to a semi-dry pulp and then stored in bins. The semi-dry material has very little odor and is trucked away periodically. Metal or glass cannot be handled by a waste pulping system and therefore these materials have to be disposed of separately. In many cases, different systems for different types of waste will have to be designed.

4

Space Requirements of Food Service Operations

The space required for each functional area of the facility is dependent upon many factors which are not constant for all types of operations. The factors involved include the number of meals to be prepared; the functions and tasks to be performed; the equipment requirements; the number of employees and corresponding workplaces required; storage for materials; and suitable space for traffic and movement. The importance of accurately evaluating these factors cannot be overemphasised. Overestimating or underestimating any of them can lead to an excess or a shortage of space for the facility.

Preliminary Space Estimation

Rules of thumb used for preliminary space estimates only. They are to be regarded as strictly tentative and subject to easy change. The "rules of thumb" are used to get a general idea of the overall size of a facility in order to make preliminary cost estimates for feasibility studies, or to determine approximate land requirements for the building. One problem with using guides and "rules of thumb" is that the figures given are usually based on existing operations and do not reflect newer methods of foodservice operation. Another difficulty is that these figures are not given for all types of foodservice operations and consequently they would be of little use for certain types of projects.

Facility Size

Depending upon the type of foodservice to be planned, a general estimate of the total building size can be obtained by relating it to the number of seats to be provided. The estimated square footage of total space per seat is given in Table 1. These figures can be related to the number of meals to be prepared by considering the turnover rate for a particular meal period. A range of space estimates is given to allow for variations in the methods of operation.

The smaller figures are used for limited menu and limited-space operations; the larger figures are suitable for operations with extensive menus and allow more spacious areas. Figures for estimating the total facility size of other types of foodservice, such as tray service, car service, or take-out service, are not available because of the great variations that exist in these types of operations.

Space for Dining Areas

The space required for dining areas is based on the number of persons to be seated at one time and the square feet of space allowed per seat. The number of persons to be seated at one time is determined by considering the total number of customers to be served for a given time period, and the turnover. Turnover refers to seat usage and is expressed by the number of times a seat will be occupied over a given time period. Turnover is usually expressed on a per-hour basis, although it can be determined on a per meal basis.

Table 1. Estimated total facility space for foodservice facilities

Type of operation	Area per seat (ft²)	(m²)
Table service	24-32	2.23-2.97
Counter service	18-24	1.86-2.60
Booth service	20-28	2.04-2.79
Cafeteria service	22-30	

The turnover is determined by estimating the average time a seat is occupied for the time period desired. For example, if the turnover is to be expressed on a per-hour basis and the average estimated time the seat is occupied is 20 minutes, the turnover is 3. If the average seat occupancy time is 30 min, then the turnover rate is 2 per hour. Determining the turnover rate per meal period is useful for determining the total seating capacity based on estimated sales volume. Turnover rates are affected by the method of serving and serving time as well as by the type of customer, menu offerings, and the dining atmosphere. Turnover rates can be increased to some extent by many design and operational factors. This is not to suggest that all facilities should be designed for high turnover rates. However, if high turnover is one of the basic objectives, then the planner and subsequent manager can use the following to accomplish this:

Use menu items that require short processing times, or use predominately preprocessed items. Provide ample production space and equipment to handle the peak periods. Use well-lighted and light-coloured painted areas for serving and dining. Arrange dining tables in close proximity to each other. Develop a somewhat uncomfortable dining seat design. Provide sufficient service personnel so guests are served promptly after they are seated. Provide for prompt clearing of the tables when a customer is finished with a course or the entire meal. Make sure guest checks are presented to customers as soon as they are finished eating. Note that a number of factors identified above are characteristic of the management policy after the facility has been built. This again emphasises the close working relationship that has to exist between the owner or manager and the planner during the planning process.

A foodservice facility designed for high turnover must also be managed for high turnover if the anticipated volume of sales is to be generated. The square feet of space allowed in the dining areas is governed by the amount of comfort desired. Crowding in dining areas is not desirable except in some quick-service fast-food operations. Most individuals would like to have sufficient elbow room and table space to enjoy their meal.

The estimates for dining areas include space for tables, chairs, aisles, and service stations. They do not allow for waiting areas, rest rooms, rather similar areas. Space requirements for these areas have to be determined separately. The size and arrangement of tables, chairs, booths, and counters selected for the dining area are important to the efficient use of the space allowed.

Space for Production Areas

The space estimates for production areas include room for all the functional areas, such as receiving, storage, preparation, cooking, and warewashing, that are required to produce the menu items. Facilities that will be processing primarily fresh items should use he higher space estimates. This allows for the additional equipment and worker space needed. The smaller figures are used for operations using preprocessed foods and require minimal production space. A suggested percentage breakdown of the production space for general table service operations is shown in Table 2.

Table 2. Estimated production space for foodservice facilities

Type of facility	Space per seat (ft^2)	(m^2)
Table service	8-12	0.74-1.11
Counter service	4-6	0.37-0.56
Booth service	6-10	0.56-0.93
Cafeteria service	8-12	0.74-1.11

Determination of Space

The problem of determining space requirements is to calculate the space needed for each of the functional areas separately. This is done by identifying and determining the pertinent variables involved for the different functional areas. It is assumed at this point that the individual workplaces and pieces of equipment for the facility have been determined and will now be grouped together.

The space required for the flow of materials and workers between the workplaces and pieces of equipment is added as needed to develop the space to allow for each function. Some of the functional areas and the variables affecting their space requirements will be given to illustrate this procedure. Computational examples are presented as applicable. Consideration of the traffic aisles is one of the common variables for all areas and is therefore included.

Traffic Aisles

Traffic aisles are used for the movement of materials and workers, and should not be confused with work aisles that provide floor space for the worker to perform the task. The primary purpose of traffic aisles is to allow easy movement between workplaces, equipment, and functional areas. Since traffic aisles are not productive space, they should be kept at a minimum both in numbers and size. In general, work aisles and traffic aisles should be separated as much as possible. This can usually be accomplished by locating traffic aisles perpendicular to the work aisles.

In some instances, combined work and traffic aisles may be used if the traffic is light and if they offer a better solution to the design problem. Traffic aisles that serve two or more functional areas will minimise the amount of space required. Placement of traffic aisles along walls and other perimeter locations is not desirable for the same reason. The width of traffic aisles is dependent upon the type of traffic to be accommodated. If it consists of only people who are not carrying anything, a minimum aisle width of 30 in. (762 mm) will allow persons to pass without difficulty.

For workers who will be carrying containers and materials or pushing mobile carts and trucks an aisle width of 24 in. (610 mm) plus the width of the container or material carried or the mobile cart width will allow enough space. For example, if one worker has to pass another worker pushing a 20-in. (508 mm) wide cart, an aisle width of 44 in. (1118 mm) (24 plus 20) would be needed. The traffic aisle widths required for special types of movement such as carrying large trays have to be sized accordingly. In those instances where a combined work and traffic aisle is needed, a minimum of 42 in. (1067 mm) is required to allow one person to pass another person at the workplace. Aisles where there are persons working in a back-to-back arrangement have to be a mimimum of 48 in. (1219 mm) wide to allow passage of people between them. An important point to remember is that the less movement required to operate the facility, the less aisle space is needed.

Space for Receiving Area

The main variables affecting the amount of space needed for the receiving function are the number, type, and size of deliveries that are to be handled at one time. Many operations can have deliveries scheduled so they will have to handle only one delivery at a time. The types of materials to be received are considered because of the variety of containers and packaging methods available. Ease of opening, checking, moving, and stackability all have a bearing on the space required. The size of deliveries to be handled may depend on the storage space available in the facility, and is determined in conjunction with storage space requirements.

Storage space in turn can be modified by the frequency of deliveries. A greater frequency of deliveries can reduce the size requirements of the receiving area as well. Therefore, storage space and receiving space requirements should be determined together after these factors have been evaluated.

Space for Storage Areas

The amount of dry, refrigerator, and freezer space required for the facility is determined by the number of days of storage to be provided for. A general recommendation for dry storage of foods is to provide space for 2-4 weeks supply, depending on the availability of the food items. The total volume of goods to be stored can be estimated as follows. First determine the number of meals for which storage is to be provided. An operation planning on serving 600 meals per day and desiring a two weeks supply will need storage for 8400 (600 meals per day ×14 days) meals. Next, estimate the weight per meal of items that will be stored in the dry storage area. This calls for an evaluation of all menu items.

A general estimate between 1/4 and 1/2 lb (0.113 and 0.227 kg) per meal may be used; it is based on a total weight estimate per average meal of 1-11/2 lb (0.454-0.680 kg). These figures are for full meals and adjustments for partial meals have to be made. If an estimate of 1/2 lb (0.227 kg) per meal is used, then the total weight to provide storage for is 4200 lb (1905 kg) (8400 meals × 0.5 lb per meal).

Then the total weight computed is divided by an average density of 45 lb per ft^3 (721 kg per m^3), which will give the total volume of goods to be stored. In this example, the total volume in cubic feet is 4200 lb = 45 lb/ ft^3 = 93.3. This indicates that space for 93.3 cubic ft (2.64 m^3) of goods, exclusive of aisle space, will be needed. If the goods are to be stored on shelves, the total square footage of shelving can be computed by considering the height to which the materials can be stored on the shelf. If the materials can be stored to a height of 1 ft, then 93.3 (93.3 ft^3 = 1 foot) ft^2 (8.67 m^2) of shelving will be needed. If a height of 11/2 ft (0.457 m) can be used, then 62.2 (93.3 =1.5) ft^2 (5.78 m^2) of shelving is required. The length of shelving is computed by dividing the square feet by the width of shelving to be used.

This same method of computation can be used for the refrigerator and freezer storage areas. The weight per meal of items that will be stored in the refrigerators and freezers will vary between 0.75 and 1 lb (0.340 and 0.454 kg). The average density of refrigerator items can be assumed to be 30 Ib/ft^3 (481 kg/m^3). Items that will be stored in freezers can be assumed to have a density of 40 Ib/ft^3 (641 kg/m^3).

The number of days of storage for refrigerator items may vary from one day to a week or more, depending on the method of operation used for the facility. Freezer items can be stored for longer periods of time and are determined by the frequency of deliveries available. An economic lot size analysis may be made to determine the optimum size of storage to provide. The analysis compares ordering, purchasing, and receiving costs to the cost of the storage.

Space for Serving Areas

Serving areas for most table service facilities are planned as a part of the main cooking area and separate space determinations are not usually needed. Additional serving stations for table service can be considered in computations for the dining area. Cafeteria operations require separate space for the serving function to allow room for the serving counter, room for guests, and room for servers.

Variables affecting the size of the serving area are the number of people to be served and the serving time allowed. Serving line rates vary from 2 to 10 persons per minute for straight-line cafeteria counters. The serving line rate is dependent on the number of choices and the number of servers. Shopping-center counter arrangements can handle up to 20 or more persons per minute. The length of cafeteria counters is determined by the variety and volume of food items to be displayed.

The space required for straight-line counters may be roughly estimated at 10-15 ft^2 (0.929-1.39 m^2) of floor space for each linear foot (0.305 m) of counter. This provides room for the counters, customer aisles, room for servers, and back-bar equipment. Shopping-center arrangements generally require 18-20 ft^2 (1.67-1.86 m^2) of floor area for each linear foot (0.305 m) of counter.

The sizing of serving facilities for cafeterias is directly related to the capacity of the dining area. Ideal design results when the flow of people from the serving facility is balanced with the seating available in the dining room. At equilibrium conditions, the flow rate of people leaving the serving areas and entering the dining area should equal the flow rate of people leaving the dining area. In other words, the number of seats provided in the dining area has a direct relationship to the rate of people leaving the serving line for a given average eating time.

For example, the maximum serving rate for a given type of serving area design can be estimated with a fair degree of accuracy if the variables affecting the serving rate are known. Another characteristic that is easily established for cafeterias is the average dining time for various types of customers or patrons. Although cafeterias may operate at different capacities during a meal period, a model can be developed to describe the peak period of operation since this is the most critical period for efficient design.

There were some symbols in model. These terms are used to describe the variables involved in the development of the model. Some of the variables described are not essential to the use of the model but are included as informational items which are helpful in determining operational characteristics of existing cafeterias. All terms are defined for the peak period of operation.

N_d = Number of persons in the dining room (this will be equated to the number of usable seats needed in dining room)

N_m = Total number of persons to be fed

N_{sa} = Number of persons in the serving area

R_1 = Rate of people entering the serving area

R_2 = Rate of people leaving the serving area (this is also considered to be the rate of people entering the dining area)

R_3 = Rate of people leaving the dining area

R_m = Feeding rate (number of people fed divided by the meal period)

R_s = Serving rate (number of people served divided by the serving period)

S = Total seats required in the dining area allowing for any vacancies that are anticipated

T_d = Time that a person spends in the dining area (sometimes referred to as dining time)

T_f = Time that the dining area is full

T_m = Meal period

T_o = Turnover of usable seats for the meal period

T_g = Serving period

T_{sa} = Time a person spends in the serving area

V = Vacancy ratio (ratio of vacant seats to total seats)

Assumptions in Model Development

The first assumption used to develop the model is that the rate of people entering the serving area is constant during the peak period of operation.

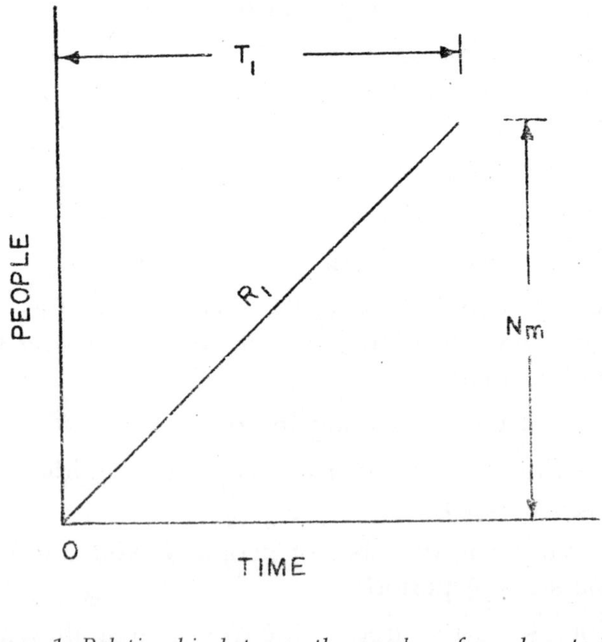

Figure 1. Relationship between the number of people entering the serving area and time.

This is a valid assumption if there is a waiting line of one or more persons at the entrance to the serving area during the entire peak period and no delays in service are encountered. This assumption also assures that the serving area will be used to its maximum capacity. The rate of people entering the serving area should be approximately the same as the arrival rate of people so the waiting time does not become excessive.

A constant rate of people entering the serving area (R_1) can be depicted by a straight line as shown in Fig. 1. The horizontal axis is used for time and the vertical axis is used for number of people. The line is drawn through the origin, which represents the beginning of the peak period. The line is drawn to a height of N_m, which represents the total number of persons that will enter the serving area. For a given rate, the time required for all the persons to enter the serving area is given by T_1. The equation for the line through the origin is given by:

$$N_m = R_1 T_1 \tag{1}$$

The second assumption used is that the rate of people leaving the serving area (or entering the dining area) is equal to the rate of people entering the serving area. This is shown by the line R_2 in Fig. 2, which is drawn parallel to line R_1. Line R_2 is also drawn to a height of N_m. The horizontal distance between lines R_1 and R_2 represent the time that a person spends in the serving area (T_{sd}). The vertical distance between the lines represents the number of people in the serving area

The horizontal distance from the origin to the point where line R_2 ends can now be defined as the serving period T_s, and represents the time elapsed from the moment the first person enters the serving area until the last person leaves the serving area. A second relationship for line R_1 can now be given by the equation:

$$R_1 = \frac{N_{sa}}{T_{sa}} \tag{2}$$

which is the slope of the line. This indicates that the rate of people entering (or leaving since $R_1 = R_2$) the serving area is equal to the number of people in the serving area divided by the time that is spent in the serving area.

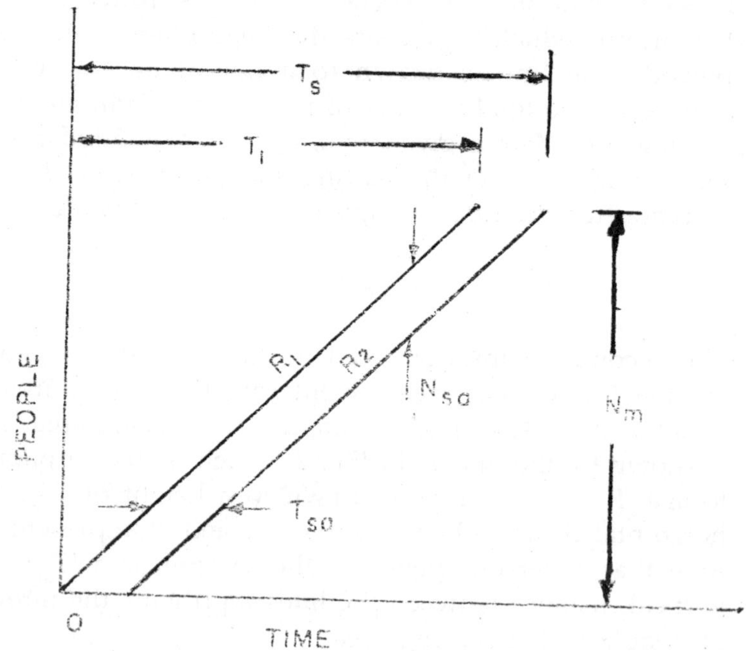

Figure 2. Graph showing the relationship for people entering and leaving the serving area.

The third assumption used for the development of the model is that the rate of people leaving the dining area is equal to the rate of people entering the dining area. The rate of people leaving the dining area is shown in Fig. 3, by line R_3, which is drawn parallel to lines R, and R_2. Line R_3 is drawn to a height of N_m.

The horizontal distance between R_2 and R_3 represents the time a person spends in the dining area (T_d). The vertical distance between lines R_2 and R_3 represents the number of people in the dining area (N_d). It is important to note that the maximum value of N_d occurs in the interval $T = T_d + T_{sa}$ and $T = T_s$.

The meal period, T_m, is shown as the horizontal distance from the origin to the point where line R_3 terminates. The relationship between T_m, T_3, and T_d can be given as:

$$T_m = T_a + T_d \tag{3}$$

At this point, the relationship between N_m and N_d can be evaluated. The turnover (T_o) in the dining area for the meal period is given by:

$$T_o = \frac{N_m}{N_d} \tag{4}$$

If $N_m = N_d$, the turnover is 1, which is the lowest turnover acceptable in cafeteria design. Indeed the highest possible turnover would be desirable as a design criterion. To assure that a turnover of less than 1 is not permitted, the model will be only valid for $N_m > N_d$. The situation where $N_m = N_d$, is shown in Fig. 4 and shows the furthest that R_3 can be drawn from the origin. For $N_m > N_d$, line R_3 will be drawn closer to the origin than shown in Fig. 4.

The relationships for the serving rate Rs and the feeding rate R_s, are described next. Using the definitions

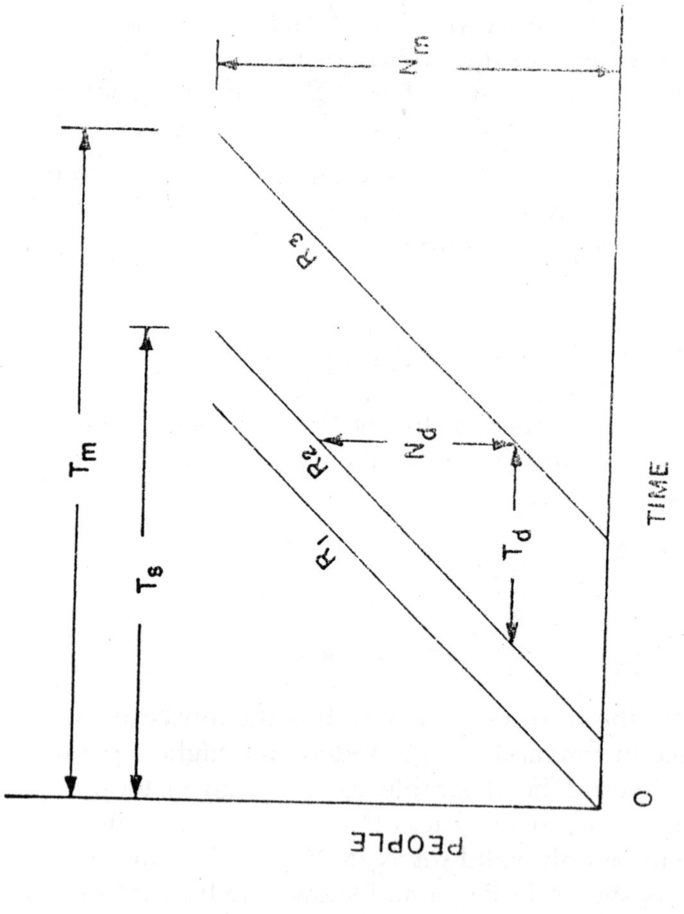

Figure 3. *Relationships for people entering and leaving the serving area and leaving the dining area.*

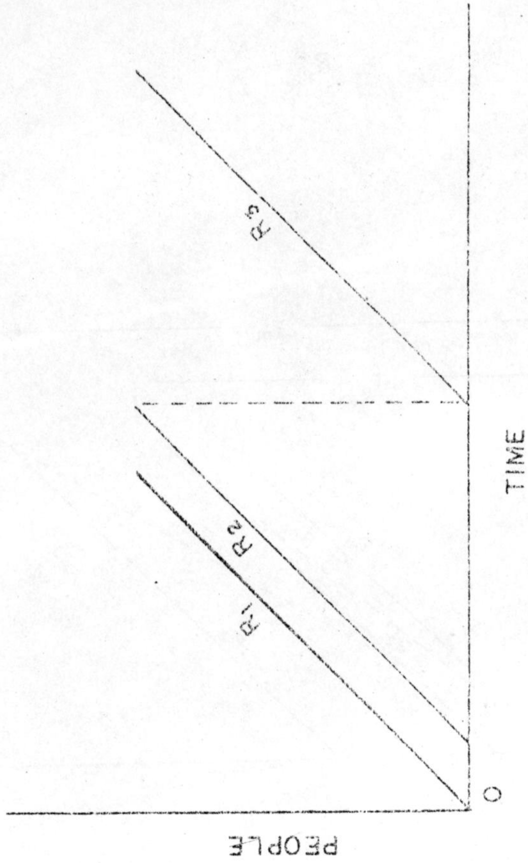

Figure 12.8. Graph showing the furthest that the line depicting people leaving the dining area can be drawn from the origin.

presented earlier, R_S and R_m are shown in Fig. 5 in relation to R_1, R_2, and R_3. The basic equation for R_s is given by:

$$R_s = \frac{N_m}{T_s} \tag{5}$$

The equation for R_m, is given by:

$$R_m = \frac{N_m}{T_m} \tag{6}$$

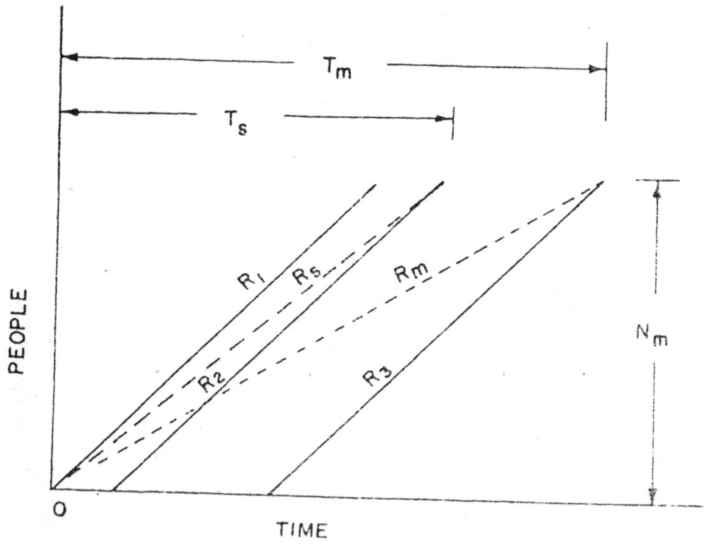

Figure 5. Relationships for determining the serving rate and the feeding rate.

These basic relationships (equations 1 through 6) were used to derive the remaining relationships for the model.

One type of cafeteria design problem exists when values or estimates of $N_{m,}$ Tm, $T_{d,}$ and N_{sa} are given. With this given information, the remaining characteristics of the cafeteria can be obtained by the following derived relationships. The time in the serving area, T_{sa}, is found by determining the horizontal distance between R_1, and R_2. In terms of time values, this distance is expressed by:

$$T_{sa} = T_s - T_1; \text{ since } T_1 = \frac{N_m}{R_1}$$

$$T_{sa} = T_s - \frac{N_m}{R_1}; \text{ and since } R_1 = \frac{N_{sa}}{T_{sa}}$$

$$T_{sa} = T_s - \frac{N_m T_{sa}}{N_{sa}}$$

The equation can be rewritten as:

$$T_{sa} + \frac{N_m T_{sa}}{N} = T_s$$

and by factoring T_{sa} gives:

$$T_{sa}\left[1 + \frac{N_m}{N_{sa}}\right] = T_s$$

and finally:

$$T_{sa} = \frac{T_s}{\left[1 + \frac{N_m}{N_{sa}}\right]} \tag{7}$$

T_{sa} can now be found in terms of T_s, N_m and N_{sa},

The next relationship derived is the equation for the maximum number of people in the dining area (N_d). N_d will be considered to be the number of usable seats to provide in the dining area. The total number of seats in the dining area will be determined by using a vacancy factor to account for unused seats caused by persons occupying only a portion of the available seats.

For example, when a party of three occupies a table for four, there will be one unused seat at the table. Vacancy factors are design decisions based on the type of customers, arrival patterns, and seating arrangement in the dining area. Since vacancy factors are not constant for all types of cafeterias, it is not included in the derivation at this time but will be included later.

N_d is found by determining the vertical distance between R_2 and R_3, As indicated earlier, the maximum value of N_d exists in the interval from $T = T_d + T_{sa}$ to $T = T_s$. In this interval the vertical distance is given by:

$$N_d = R_2 T_d$$

R_2 can be expressed by the slope of the line as:

$$R_2 = \frac{N_m + N_{sa}}{T_m - T_d}$$

Substituting for R_2 in the equation for N_d, gives:

$$N_d = \left[\frac{N_m + N_{sa}}{T_m - T_d}\right] T_d$$

which can be rewritten as:

$$N_d = \frac{N_m + N_{sa}}{\left[\dfrac{T_m}{T_d} - 1\right]} \tag{8}$$

Equation 8 gives the maximum number of people in the dining area and is equated to the number of usable seats to provide. To allow for vacancies, the total number of seats to provide is given by the relationship:

$$S = \frac{N_d}{(1 - V)}$$

where V is the vacancy ratio expressed as a decimal. A relationship between R_2 and R_8 can be developed by using the following terms to describe the slope of line R_2:

$$R_2 = \frac{N_m}{T_s - T_{sa}}; \text{ since } N_m = R_s T_s$$

$$R_2 = \frac{R_s T_s}{T_s - T_{sa}}$$

Dividing the numerator and denominator of the right-hand side of the equation by T_s results in the following:

$$R_2 = \frac{R_s}{\left[1 - \dfrac{T_{sa}}{T_s}\right]}$$

The final relationship developed is the time that the dining room is full, as shown below:

$$T_f = T_s - T_d - T_{sa}$$

The equations developed may be used to make the design decisions needed in the planning of a new cafeteria, as shown by the following examples. The first example assumes that the following information is given or estimated:

N_m = 200 persons

T_m = 120 min.

T_d = 30 min.

N_{sa} = 10 people

V = 10%

The determination of the variables affecting the design is shown below.

$$T_s = T_m - T_d, \text{ (from equation 3)}$$

$$T_s = 120 - 30 = 90 \text{ min.}$$

$$R_s = \frac{N_m}{T_s} = \frac{200}{90} = 2.2 \text{ persons/min.}$$

$$R_m = \frac{N_m}{T_m} = \frac{200}{120} = 1.7 \text{ persons/min.}$$

$$T_{sa} = \frac{T_s}{\left[1 + \frac{N_m}{N_{sa}}\right]} = \frac{90}{\left[1 + \frac{200}{10}\right]} = 4.3 \text{ min.}$$

$$N_d = \frac{N_m + N_{sa}}{\left[\frac{T_m}{T_d} - 1\right]} = \frac{200 + 10}{\left[\frac{120}{30} - 1\right]} = 70 \text{ people}$$

$$S = \frac{N_d}{(1 - V)} = \frac{70}{(1 - 0.10)} = 77.8 \text{ or } 78 \text{ seats}$$

$$R_2 = \frac{N_{sa}}{T_{sa}} = \frac{10}{4.3} = 2.3 \text{ persons/min.}$$

$$T_o = \frac{N_m}{N_d} = \frac{200}{70} = 2.9 \text{ for the meal period}$$

$$T_f = T_s - T_d - T_{sa} = 90 - 30 - 4.3 = 55.7 \text{ min.}$$

Arrival Rates of Customers

If the arrival rate of customers to the cafeteria can be determined can be equated to the rate of people entering the serving area (R_1). An example of this type of computation for a different design problem is shown next.

Given:
R_1 = 5 persons/min.
N_m = 300 people
T_d = 20 min.
N_{sa} = 8 persons
V = 15%

Computations:

$$N_d = \frac{N_m}{T_o} = \frac{200}{2.5} = 80 \text{ persons}$$

$$S = \frac{N_d}{(1 - V)} = \frac{80}{(1 - 0.10)} = 89 \text{ seats}$$

$$R_2 = \frac{N_d}{T_d} = \frac{80}{30} = 2.7 \text{ persons/min.}$$

$$T_{sa} = \frac{N_{sa}}{R_2} = \frac{10}{2.7} = 3.7 \text{ persons/min.}$$

$$T_s = T_{sa}\left[1 + \frac{N_m}{N_{sa}}\right] = 3.7\left[1 + \frac{200}{10}\right] = 78 \text{ min.}$$

$$T_m = T_s + T_d = 78 + 30 = 108 \text{ min.}$$

$$R_s = \frac{N_m}{T_s} = \frac{200}{78} = 2.6 \text{ persons/min.}$$

$$R_m = \frac{N_m}{T_m} = \frac{200}{108} = 1.9 \text{ persons/min.}$$

Evaluation of Existing Cafeterias

The model may be used to evaluate existing cafeterias, as

shown by the following example. In this case the total number of seats in the dining area (S) and the size of the serving area (which determines N_{sa}) are fixed. Then for any given T_m, T_d, and V, the following calculations can be made.

Given: S = 150 seats
N_{sa} = 12 persons
T_m = 60 min.
T_d = 15 min.
V = 10%

Computations:

$$N_d = S\,(1 - V) = 150\,(1 - 0.10) = 135 \text{ people}$$

$$R_1 = \frac{N_d}{T_d} = \frac{135}{15} = 9 \text{ persons/min.}$$

$$T_{sa} = \frac{N_{sa}}{R_1} = \frac{12}{9} = 1.3 \text{ min.}$$

$$T_s = T_m - T_d = 60 - 15 = 45 \text{ min.}$$

$$R_s = R_1\left[1 - \frac{T_{sa}}{T_s}\right] = 9\left[1 - \frac{1.3}{45}\right] = 8.7 \text{ persons/min.}$$

$$N_m = R_s T_s = 8.7\,(45) = 392 \text{ persons}$$

$$R_m = \frac{N_m}{T_m} = \frac{392}{60} = 6.5 \text{ persons/min.}$$

$$T_o = \frac{N_m}{N_d} = \frac{392}{135} = 2.9$$

A variation of the above example is to determine what meal period would be required to accommodate a given number of people to be fed. To illustrate, the meal period for the above problem when N_m = 500 will be shown. Note that the values of N_d, R_1, and T_{sa} do not change. The remaining computations are shown below.

$$T_s = \frac{[N_m + N_{sa}]}{R_1} = \frac{[500 + 12]}{9} = 56.9 \text{ min.}$$

$$T_m = T_s + T_d = 56.9 + 15 = 71.9 \text{ min.}$$

$$R_s = \frac{N_m}{T_s} = \frac{500}{56.9} = 8.8 \text{ persons/min.}$$

$$R_m = \frac{N_m}{T_m} = \frac{500}{71.9} = 7 \text{ persons/min.}$$

$$T_o = \frac{N_m}{N_d} = \frac{500}{135} = 3.7$$

The computations show that the meal period would have to be 71.9 min. in order to accommodate the 500 people. The analytical model described for cafeteria operations is a very useful tool for planners. It allows for the manipulation of factors so that any design objective may be attained. Since the model was based on a peak period of operation, the resulting design represents the most efficient facility possible. Operators of existing cafeterias may also use the model to describe more fully the operating characteristics of their facility. This may lead to changes that could increase the efficiency of their cafeteria.

SPACE CALCULATION IN DINING AREAS

Calculating the space requirements for dining areas can be difficult because of the many choices available. For example, the final space required for a dining room is dependent upon the following variables:

1. Types of seating to be provided:
   a. Tables and chairs

   b. Booths
   c. Counters
   d. Banquettes
   e. Combinations
2. Table sizes desired
3. Table shapes desired
4. Pattern of table arrangements
5. Aisle space desired
6. N- umber of service stations needed

A suggested approach that allows a planner to evaluate these variables and their effect on the dining space per seat is the modular concept. For this situation the module contains space for the table, the seats, and the appropriate share of the service and access aisles. The modular concept enables designers first to evaluate the space requirements for different choices that may be made before reaching their final decisions.

The following example will illustrate this concept for a dining room that will use tables and chairs only. The first step in the modular concept is to select the size and shape of table to be considered. This is done in relation to the customer, the menu, the type of service, and the type of atmosphere desired in the dining room.

The second step is to select the aisle spaces to be used. Aisle space in dining areas may be divided into service aisles and access aisles. Service aisles usually range from 2.5 ft (0.762 m) minimum for a limited menu operation to as wide as 4.5 ft (1.37 m) for a dining room featuring cart service or table side food preparation. Access aisles are provided to allow people to get into and out of the chairs easily. Thus the type of customer, size of chairs, and the desired atmosphere (crowded versus spacious) are the critical factors in selecting the access aisles. Access aisles are generally 1.5 ft (0.457 m) to 2 ft (0.610 m) wide as a minimum. Combined service and access aisles or aisles for cafeterias where people carry their own trays are usually sized from 3 ft (0.914 m) to 4.5ft. (1.37 m).

Having selected the table size and shape and the desired aisle space, the next step is to consider possible table arrangement patterns. Square or round tables may be arranged into a rectangular or diagonal pattern, as shown in Fig. 6. The diagonal pattern is more efficient in the use of space than the rectangular pattern.

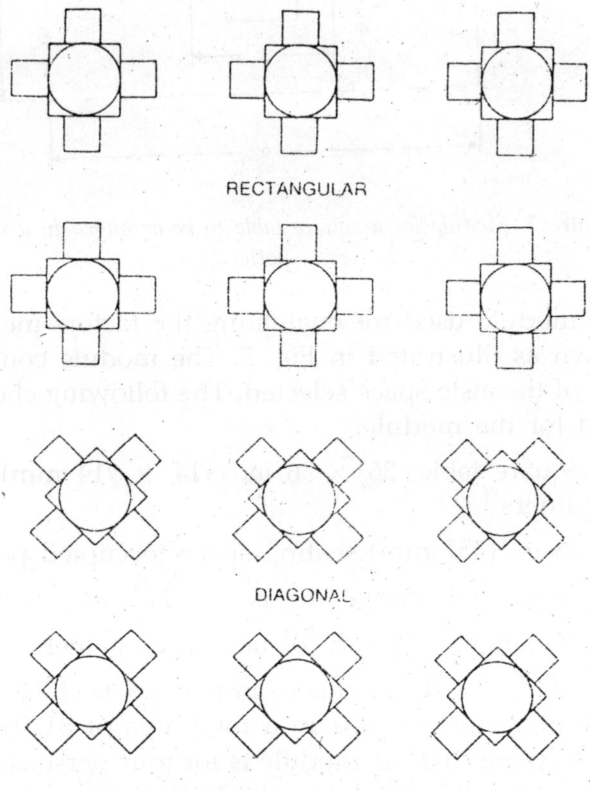

Figure 6. Rectangular and diagonal placement of tables

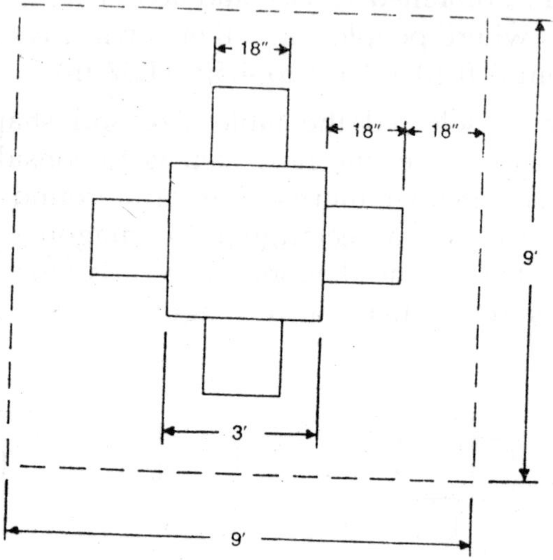

Figure 7. Module for a square table to be arranged in a rectangular pattern

The module used for evaluating the factors mentioned is drawn as illustrated in Fig. 7. The module contains one-half of the aisle space selected. The following choices were used for the module:

1. Square table, 36 × 36 in. (914 × 914 mm), for four diners
2. 18 in. (457 mm) seating space (occupied position)
3. Combined service and access aisle of 3 ft (0.914 m)
4. Rectangular pattern of table arrangement

The module size for this example is 9 ft (2.74 m) by 9 ft (2.74 m), which results in a total area of 81 ft^2 (7.52 m^2). Considering that the module is for four persons, the space per seat for this module is 20.25 ft^2 (1.88 m^2)/seat. If this module were to be used for a dining room with 100 seats, the total area required would be 2025 ft^2 (188 m^2). The module for a diagonal pattern of table arrangement using the same choices for the table size, seat space, and aisle space is shown in Fig. 8. The size of the module for the diagonal pattern is 8 ft in. (2.54 m) by 8 ft 4 in. (2.54 m), which gives a total area of 69.44 ft^2 (6.45 m^2). The space per seat is 17.36 ft^2 (1.61 m^2)/seat, which is 2.89 ft^2 (0.27 m^2) less than for the rectangular pattern. For the 100 seat dining room, the diagonal pattern would require 1736 ft^2 (161 m^2), which is 289 ft^2 (26.8 m^2) less than the rectangular pattern.

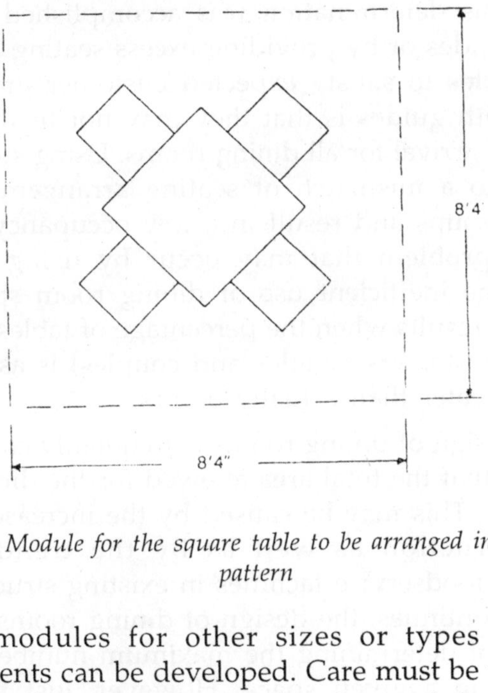

Figure 8. Module for the square table to be arranged in a diagonal pattern

Similar modules for other sizes or types of seating arrangements can be developed. Care must be taken when using different size tables so that the modules developed for each size table are compatible at least on one side. For example, when tables for twos and tables for fours are to be used, the modules can be adjusted by selecting table shapes or sizes that give the same module dimension along one axis. This would allow a mixing of the tables without affecting the pattern of aisle ways in the dining area.

Seating Capacity and Occupancy

An important aspect of foodservice facilities planning that is becoming more important, especially for table service operations, is the determination of the number of each type of table to plan for the dining room. Basically this involves the determination of how many tables for two, four, six, and so on should be used in a given type of facility. In the past, this determination was accomplished by using standard guides or by providing excess seating at various sizes of tables to satisfy expected customer groups. The problem with guides is that they may not fit the pattern of customer arrival for all dining rooms. Using such guides may lead to a mismatch of seating arrangements with customer groups and result in a low occupancy of seats. A related problem that may occur by using standard guides is the inefficient use of dining room space. This inefficiency results when the percentage of tables for small groups of customers (singles and couples) is assumed to be much greater than actually occurs.

The design of dining rooms is frequently complicated by the fact that the total area allowed for the dining room is restricted. This may be caused by the increased cost of new construction as well as by the trend toward developing foodservice facilities in existing structures. As this trend continues, the design of dining rooms becomes a problem of determining the maximum number of seats to provide in a given space. However, just providing maximum seating capacity may not be the best solution if it results in a low occupancy of seats. This may occur when tables for two are occupied by singles or if tables for four or six are used to seat smaller groups. The ideal solution to the problem is to provide maximum seating capacity that matches customer group sizes and therefore results in a minimum of vacant seats.

The most important data required to solve this type of design problem is obviously an accurate knowledge of customer groups arriving for a given type of foodservice operation. For some operations, determination of the arrival of different sized customer groups for more than one meal period may be required. Although this type of data can be obtained for existing operations when a dining room is remodelled, it has to be estimated for proposed foodservice facilities.

5

Food Service Equipment

Food service equipment are tools used for the cooking and preparation of food, cleaning of utensils and dinnerware. A food service without utensils is unthinkable and a well-equipped food service is every manager's dream. But since food service managers are also individuals, a list of food service equipment and utensils which may suit one may not suit another. However there are certain essential items that every food service needs and as such are identified by the number of times they are used.

Different pieces of foos service equipment exist for every purpose. While setting up a new foos service, certain amount of time and thought has to be given in choosing and buying equipment and utensils where utmost importance should be given to quality. Modern food service establishments are equipped with many efficient labour-saving devices. Machines make tasks such as chopping, shredding and pureeing easier and less time consuming. A food service appliance is a major investment, not only in the initial purchase cost but also in the use, care, energy consumption, and maintenance for the lifetime of the appliance.

Kitchen Stoves

A kitchen stove is used to cook food, and refers to a device which has both burners on the top (also known as a cooktop or range or hob) and an oven. Modern stoves are typically considered a basic appliance in homes in developed nations. Along with the refrigerator, a stove is typically located in the kitchen room.

Many modern stoves typically have from three to six burners or hotplates of various sizes and power levels, an oven, and knobs for controlling heat on burners, which may be located on the backsplash, on the cooktop, or on the front of the stove closest to one's hips. Middle to high-end models also may feature locking mechanisms for the oven door, convection cooking, automatic cleaning mechanisms that raise the oven temperature to over 260 degrees Celsius and reduce accumulated food spills to ash, one or more timers, a digital display, and may even be programmable such that they start and stop heating at preset times.

Halogen Cooking System: The halogen cooking system is one of the newest cooking units available. Its tungsten halogen lamps appear to produce virtually instantaneous heat and light. The halogen unit surface is made of vitro-ceramic. This new, smooth surface is also used for some of the induction cooking systems.

Induction Cooking System: The induction cooking system is quite new to many consumers. It is fast, safe, and energy efficient. Target temperatures can be instantly achieved and very low temperatures can be easily maintained to eliminate burning. The cooking surface stays cool, so less heat escapes into the kitchen. Only the cookware, which must be magnetic, and the food get hot-not the entire cooking surface.

Solid-disk Cooking System: The solid-disk cooking system is somewhat new and currently very popular. European design, ease of cleaning, and evenness of cooking are some of the reasons for its popularity. The disk requires frequent application of a special cleaning treatment to keep it looking new. Since the solid disk is made of cast iron, it is slow to heat-up, cooks evenly, and retains heat well. Energy can be saved by turning the element off and using the retained heat to complete cooking.

Convertible Cooking System: The convertible cooking system stoves can be custom designed simply by unplugging a module and plugging in a different one. There are modules for induction, halogen, solid-disk, conven-tional-coil, and glass ceramic cooking. Extra modules are also available for deep-fat frying, griddling, grilling, barbecuing, and wok cooking. Convertible cooking surfaces work well in open kitchen areas because an overhead exhaust unit is not needed due to the presence of down-draft ventilation systems.

Pilotless Gas Cooking System: Pilotless gas stoves are relatively new. Elimination of the continually burning pilot light results in big energy savings. It also keeps the kitchen cooler. The new gas stoves are easier to clean. On many of the new gas stoves, the top lifts up or off so burners can be easily removed and cleaned. In addition, the knobs, burner bowls, and cookware supports can be easily removed for cleaning.

Beverage Can Stoves: A beverage can stove is a homemade, ultra-light backpacking stove. The simple design is made entirely from cans and burns denatured alcohol. Countless variations on the basic design exist. Pepsi cans are often used because they have a bottom shape that lends itself to securing the stove's inner wall, and because of this the stoves are sometimes called Pepsi can stoves. The Pepsi can stove weighs 0.4 oz (10 g) and will boil two cups of water in five minutes with two tablespoons of fuel. Total weight, including a windscreen/ stand can be less than one ounce (30 g). Due to the low weight compared to commercial stoves and their fuel canisters, backpackers can save about one pound (450 g) of pack weight with this stove. This advantage may be lost on long hiking trips however, because the stove is less efficient and requires more fuel, especially when cooking for more than one person.

The stove is made from two aluminum can bottoms. An inner wall is cut and rolled from can material. A ring of holes is pierced into the top with a pin. Parts are glued with high temperature epoxy, or sealed with thermal foil tape. Total height is less than two inches (50 mm), though dimensions can be increased to hold more fuel or decreased to take up even less space. The choice of aluminum has several advantages; light weight, low cost, and good thermal conductivity to aid vaporisation of fuel. Alternative construction materials have been used, including stoves made of tin cans such as cat food tins, tuna cans, and juice cans—the basic design is very similar. Windscreens/stands can be fabricated from tin cans, cut to size and with ventilation holes added.

The stove is designed for one or two people. When used to cook larger meals, it is less efficient than a more powerful stove that delivers more heat to a pot. This is because a longer cooking time is required, during which more heat is lost to the surroundings. To use the stove, a small amount of fuel is poured into the stove and ignited. The pot is then placed above the stove, on a windscreen or stand. The flame is small at first, only burning from the inner chamber. Once the fuel has warmed up, requiring about one minute, its vapour will pass through the perforations and form a ring of flame.

Portable stoves: A portable stove is a stove specially designed to be portable and lightweight, such as for camping. There are several main types based on the type of fuel used:

— Simple single-burner stoves, often without any controls at all, using solid or liquid fuel which is placed in the burner before ignition.

— Single-burner stoves using volatile liquid fuel in a pressurised burner-tank combination.

— Single or multi burner bottled gas stoves, providing controls for the heat setting similar to a kitchen cooktop.

— Gravity-fed spirit stoves, with priming pans.

Simple single-burner designs: The simplest stove is a burner that contains the fuel, and which once lit burns until either it is snuffed or the fuel is exhausted. The rise in the popularity of extreme light-weight equipment for extended backpacking, and the increasing restrictions on the use of campfires in most wilderness areas, have made these small stoves extremely popular. The two most popular of these are the solid fuel stove, using Hexamine tablets, and the liquid fuelled stove using methylated spirits. Both types are available commercially. There are also many designs published for similar home-built stoves, like the Pepsi can stove.

While solid-fuelled stoves may be refuelled while burning with care, with a liquid-fuelled stove it would be reckless to attempt this. Both solid alcohol fuel and stoves for using it are produced by Esbit, and fuel is produced by several other makers. While most brands of firelighters can be used in such stoves, some types will produce a troublesome residue that may be impossible to remove from cookware, and will taint any food exposed to the flame or fumes. One popular make of simple liquid-fuelled stove is the Trangia, available in many different models from a single bare burner to an integrated expedition cooking system. Some of these come with a sealing cover, allowing the burner to be packed while containing fuel.

Pressurised burner stoves: There is some controversy over the invention of the pressurised burner. Most have given the credit to F.W. Linqvist, who was granted a patent for a kerosene-fuelled burner in the late 1880s and went on to develop the Primus brand name of stove into a market leader. However, some have suggested that he bought the design. The Primus stoves and their imitators were a significant advance over previous designs that had used a wick to supply liquid fuel to the burner by capillary action. Instead the Primus burner vaporised the fuel in a loop of pipe, and used this to both supply the fuel to the burner as a gas and to maintain pressure in the fuel tank. Initial pressure was provided by a small hand-operated pump. It was also necessary to pre-heat the burner with methylated spirits. This burner design was also successfully adapted to portable lamps, lighthouse lamps and blowtorches.

Pressurised burner stoves are now available to burn almost any volatile, inflammable liquid, including alcohol, diesel or other motor fuels, kerosene, jet propellant, and many others. Work is proceeding on vegetable-oil burners. Some can burn multiple fuels or even mixtures. Some require special low-residue stove fuel, others are either designed to resist clogging or to be easily and regularly cleaned of the residue. Most provide some control over the amount of heat produced. Some fuels permit preheating with the fuel, others require use of a more volatile fuel, such as methylated spirit or alcohol priming paste, for preheating the burner.

Most provide an integrated pump for initial pressurisation, others require the use of a separate pump, while a few need no pump but pressurise themselves when the burner is preheated. Although heavier than the simpler designs and more complex to maintain and operate, these stoves can heat food more quickly, and as standard issue to many units in the second world war they enjoyed a large base of competent users in the years immediately following. Another advantage is that hydrocarbon fuels have a higher heat content weight for weight than alcohol fuels, so for extended expeditions the weight advantage of alcohol-fuelled stoves is reduced or even reversed.

Gas-cartridge stoves and refillable gas-bottle stoves: The greatest variety in designs is in this category. They include gas-cartridge stoves and refillable gas-bottle stoves. In most of these the gas is stored as a liquid under pressure, but vaporises immediately it leaves the storage bottle and so arrives at the burner as a gas. Smaller, lighter designs tend to use non-refillable gas cartridges containing butane, propane or a mixture of hydrocarbons. There is little compatibility between different makers and systems, and cartridges for older stoves are often unobtainable. In addition, the single-use cartridges are considered objectionable by some on environmental grounds. Refillable gas bottles are heavier and tend to be used on larger stoves intended for car-camping or expedition base camps. However a great variety of gas-fired stoves is available, some integrating the gas cylinder, some connecting it by a hose.

Gravity-fed spirit stoves: The traditional "spirit stove" still found in many pleasure boats is a unique design, largely replaced by gas stoves but still with a following. It consists of a tank that supplies methylated spirit under gravity to the burner or burners, where it is vaporised and burned. Around each burner is a priming pan used to preheat the burner. To light the stove, the burner is first turned on to allow a small amount of fuel to pass through the burner and collect as a liquid in the priming pan. The burner is then turned off, and the fuel ignited to preheat the burner. When the fuel in the pan is almost all gone, the burner is turned on again, and fuel passes into the burner where it is vaporised and passes through the jets. These stoves look and even sound a bit like pressurised-burner stoves, but the fuel tank is under no pressure. They remain popular for small boats owing to the minimal fire risk they pose in a confined space.

Liquid-fuel and Gas-fuel stoves: Most stoves can use either liquid or gas fuel, but not both (One exception is Primus Omni/Multi-Fuel). Gas-fuel stoves are simpler to operate than liquid fuelled stoves. The gas, being already pressurised, flows from the fuel canister into the burner, where it ignites, in the same manner as a domestic kitchen stove. Liquid-fuel stoves are more complex because the liquid fuel must be vaporised prior to burning. To accomplish this, the stove design brings the fuel line containing the liquid fuel near the flame of the burner. The heat from the flames converts the liquid fuel to a gas before it reaches the burner, where it mixes with air and is ignited. Stoves operating with liquid fuels must be heated or primed before the burner is turned on.

Many stoves require the operator to open the fuel valve briefly without igniting the fuel, so that it flows into a small pan. This small quantity of fuel is then lit and allowed to burn down. When the fuel valve is opened again, the fuel vaporises from the heat of the pan. Some stoves do not have this apparatus, and must be preheated by the application of an external heat source such as a solid fuel block. In many stoves, the priming pressure is generated by a small hand pump that forces air into the fuel container. As the fuel is consumed, the pressure decreases according to Boyle's Law, so the pump must be operated occasionally during use to maintain steady stove operation. Liquid fuel stoves are the most popular for backpacking in United States.

Liquid fuel costs less than gas fuel generally. Some forms of fuel, such as kerosene or fuel oil, are readily available worldwide. Disadvantages to liquid fuelled stoves include they require priming, hence some skill is needed to operate them properly. Using liquid fuel stove in a tent is difficult or even dangerous. The fuel does not burn as cleanly as gas fuelled stoves. Soot builds up on cooking vessels eventually. Spilt liquid fuel poses a fire hazard, and can soil equipment. The odour of the fuel may also attract dangerous wild animals.

Gaseous fuels have many advantages; the fuel burns cleanly. They are quite simple to use, just adjust the fuel flow with a valve and light the burner. Since the gasious fuel quickly dissipates, the fire hazard associated with leaking fuel is reduced. Safety is also increased because there is no priming. Gas fuel bottles of a particular make may be widely available in some countries but not in others, so international travellers' have to be particularly careful. Some disadvantages of gas fuel are the difficulty of transferring fuel from one container to another and the difficulty of accurately gauging how much fuel remains in a container.

Gas fuel is somewhat less efficient than liquid fuel, meaning more fuel volume is required for the same heat output. Gas fuelled stoves usually do not operate well in colder temperatures. Butane in particular, does not vaporise well at low temperatures which makes stoves fuelled with butane unsuitable for cold weather camping. Boiling point of butane under normal pressure is -1°C and under this temperature butane cannot be used as a fuel for gas stove. The temperature where use of butane becomes impractical is even higher (around 5°C). Propane-butane-isobutane mixtures used in most containers are suitable to temperatures of -10°C. Pure propane boils at -42°C which is the actual limit of usability of propane stoves. Gas fuel canisters tend to be heavier than liquid-fuel bottles, because it must be stored under greater pressure. When a canister runs out, it may have to be treated as hazardous waste. Canisters tend to deteriorate and leak if stored for several years.

Solid-fuel stoves: A quantity of liquid fuel sufficient to cook a meal, if simply placed in a container and ignited, would burn violently and consume itself in a matter of seconds, and a similar quantity of gas fuel would simply explode. The primary design principle of stoves that use these fuels is to provide a steady flame and prevent the fuel's escape. Solid fuel, however, is more manageable. A solid-fuel stove may consist of no more than a metal plate to hold the fuel, a set of legs to keep it out of contact with the ground, and some supports for the cooking vessel. This design is highly scalable, and may be used for anything from tiny backpacking stoves to large portable woodstoves.

While admirably simple, solid fuel has many disadvantages. First of all, its burn rate may be controlled only by varying the amount of fuel placed on the fire, while fluid fuels may be controlled precisely with valves. Second, no solid fuel burns completely. It produces considerable amounts of ash and soot, which soil both the stove and the cooking vessels. Some of the chemical energy of the fuel remains locked up in the ash and soot, so solid fuel releases less heat, gram for gram. Firewood may often be used in solid-fuel stoves, but manufactured fuels are also available. One type is sold in the form of small blocks, on the order of a centimeter in size. Sterno is a viscous fluid that is also used in solid-fuel stoves. Simple stoves are sometimes used in ice houses and large tents, both to provide warmth and for cooking. They burn wood, and have a small flue used to exhaust the smoke. When used in tents, they are used in a larger tent made of fabric that does not burn readily, and are most often used in base camps that move infrequently.

Ovens

One of the newest features found in ovens is convection cooking. It is available in portable, full-size, free-standing, and built-in wall ovens. In convection ovens, a fan blows the heated air over and around food, increasing the rate of moisture evaporation and thus decreasing cooking time.

The oven temperature can be reduced 25 to 50 degrees when cooking with convection because of the air circulation and more even cooking. Shorter cooking times and lower temperatures add up to important energy and dollar savings. Because convection ovens use forced-air for cooking, noise level is a consideration. It should be low enough to not be irritating. Some manufacturers are making combination ovens as an option to conventional gas or electric ovens. These combination ovens allow microwave-convection, microwaveconventional, or convection-conventional cooking in a single large oven.

Microwave Oven

Microwave energy is a natural phenomenon that occurs when electric current flows through a conductor. Microwaves are a form of electromagnetic radiation that is very similar to sunlight and radio waves. The microwaves do not heat glass, ceramic, and plastic containers. One advantage of microwaving is that small amounts of food can be heated very quickly, making it useful for reheating leftovers. A disadvantage of microwaving is that food which is microwaved does not undergo some of the chemical reactions, such as browning, that make the food both visually attractive and give it a different flavour. Primitive microwave ovens often do not cook the food evenly, leading to a concern that bacteria easily killed by more traditional cooking methods may survive the quick cooking time in "cold spots", though the food item as a whole is cooked to a safe average temperature. This can be overcome by leaving the food to stand for a few minutes when cooking is completed. Some high-end microwave ovens are combined with a convection oven; they cook the food using microwaves and hot air simultaneously to achieve both the fast cooking time and the browning effect.

Using a microwave for cooking a large food mass is difficult due to limited penetration of microwaves. However, microwave ovens are used in some fast food chains, and special microwave bags are available for cooking fowl or large joints of meat. Professional chefs generally recommend using microwaves for a limited set of tasks, including melting fats (such as butter) and chocolate, cooking grains like oatmeal and grits, cooking rice, thawing frozen meats and vegetables before cooking by other methods, and quickly reheating already-cooked foods. A common myth is that a microwave oven cooks from the centre of the food outward. However, most foods only have their outermost inch heated by the microwaves, and the rest of the food is heated via conduction. Similarly, foods with both air and water content allow the microwaves to penetrate fully, heating the entire item with the microwave radiation.

Using a microwave to boil liquids is potentially dangerous, due to the possibility of superheating. In a microwave, liquids can be raised quickly to a temperature above the boiling point before major bubbles form, especially if the liquid is purified and in a very clean glass vessel. When a liquid in a superheated state is disturbed, it can suddenly and unexpectedly boil violently, leading to a risk of scalding. This effect is rare, even for scientists who try to deliberately recreate it, and any seed whatsoever for boiling is likely to prevent the problem.

Boiling water with, for instance, a teabag already in it will prevent any dangers by providing a seed, as will using a mug that is not perfectly clean. The risk greatly increases when the liquid has already been boiled once in the same container. This situation can occur if the user of the oven boiled the liquid once, forgot about it, then came back later to boil it again. The first time the liquid boils, the seed bubbles are used up and largely eliminated from the liquid as it cools down. When the liquid is heated again, the lack of seed bubbles allows superheating, and creates the risk of a steam explosion when the liquid's surface is disturbed. Placing something in the liquid before heating can mostly alleviate this risk.

If you are planning to mix something with the liquid you are heating, such as tea or hot chocolate, adding it before heating will ensure that the liquid boils properly. Otherwise, placing a wood object, for instance a chopstick, in the water before heating will also work. All that is necessary to prevent superheating is the presence of seed bubbles, so any liquid that has been allowed to sit undisturbed for a period of time is more prone to superheating. Care should be taken when removing heated liquids from a microwave. Make sure that the hands are protected from possible liquid boil-over, place the container on a level, heat-proof surface, and stir liquid with a warm spoon. Also, never add powdered substances to the container taken from the microwave, due to the addition of a large amount of seed bubbles and the potential for violent, spontaneous boiling. It is advised that the liquid be poured slowly into another container that already contains the powder.

Metal objects, such as metal utensils, in a microwave oven can lead to dangerous situations. Metals do not absorb microwaves effectively. Instead, metals reflect microwaves, thereby preventing the latter from reaching the food. If the microwaves are not absorbed inside the oven, the oven can be damaged by electrical arcs and overheating of the microwave source. Thin metal layers, such as metal foil and mugs with metal trim, can melt or burn due to the strong electrical currents that are generated in metal objects. However, small solid metal objects, such as spoons, in combination with a large amount of absorbing food or liquid, normally do not lead to problems. With wireless computer networks gaining in popularity, microwaves can disrupt wireless network transmissions because the microwave creates radio waves at about 2.4 GHz. This is about the same frequency that 802.11 wireless networks use, so microwaves in use may interfere with network signals, as the specific frequency varies slightly.

A microwave oven is a kitchen appliance employing microwave radiation primarily to cook or heat food. A microwave oven consists of:

— a magnetron,
— a magnetron control circuit,
— a waveguide, and
— a cooking chamber

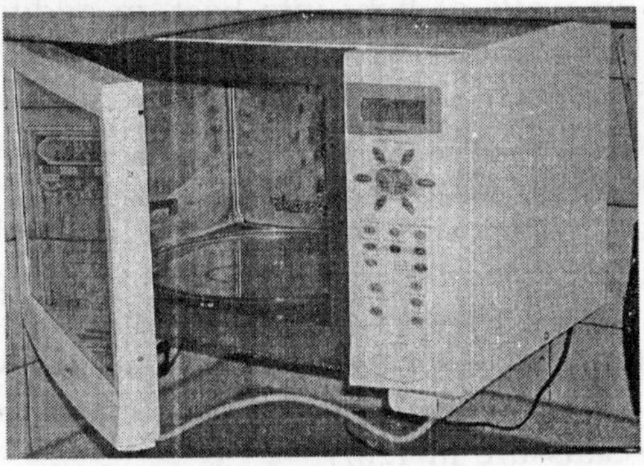

Microwave oven

A microwave oven does not convert all electrical energy into microwaves. A typical consumer microwave oven could consume 1100 W, and deliver 700 W of microwave power. The remaining 400 W are dissipated as heat by components of the oven. The main source of energy loss is the magnetron tube which is much less than 100% efficient at generating microwave output from the power source. Lesser amounts of power are consumed by the oven lamp, AC power transformer losses, magnetron cooling fan, food turntable motor and control circuits. This waste heat does not end up in the food but is mostly expelled from the cooling vents on the oven and heats the air in the kitchen. Most of the actual microwave power will end up heating the food inside the oven, unless the microwave oven is loaded with a very small amount of absorbing food.

Solar Oven

A solar oven or solar cooker is a way of harnessing the sun's power to cook food. A metal box forms the simplest solar oven. A set of large mirrors or a large Fresnel lens to focus sunlight to a single point may also be added. On a sunny day a black baking tray or cooking pot can convert thousands of watts of light into heat, in addition to any infra-red. Temperatures in a typical oven can reach 400 degrees F (200°C). Apart from the obvious need for sunlight and the need to aim the solar oven before use, using a solar oven is not substantially different from a regular oven. However since they use no fuel they are free to run. Humanitarian organisations are promoting their use worldwide to help slow deforestation and desertification caused by the need for firewood with which to cook. The first known western solar oven was built by Horace de Saussure in 1767.

The available designs of solar ovens fall into three main categories: the box, parabolic, and panel designs. The feature common to each oven design is the shiny reflective surface that directs the sun's rays onto a dark cooking vessel. Each category has advantages when compared on their heating ability, ease of construction, ease and safety of use.

Box cookers: Box cookers are the most common type made for personal use. Despite the name "box" cooker, they are made in both circular and rectangular shapes. Box cooker consist of an enclosed inner box covered with clear glass or plastic, a reflector, and insulation. There is a wide variety of patterns and plans that can be adapted to work with available materials. While they do not heat quickly, they provide slow, even cooking. Box cookers are very easy and safe to use, and fairly easy to construct.

Parabolic cookers: Parabolic cookers reach higher temperatures and cook more quickly than solar box cookers, but are harder to make and use. Most commercial ovens are a form of parabolic cooker. Parabolic cookers require more precision to focus the sunlight on the cooking vessel. If the sunlight is not focused exactly on the cooking vessel, the food will not cook. When the parabolic oven is used, the temperature must be watched so the vessel does not overheat, burning the food. The risk of burns and eye injury is greater with homemade parabolic designs. While they provide excellent results when used correctly, they are not easy to build at home and require great care to use.

Convection Oven

Convection ovens use heated air that is forced into the oven by fans located in the back of the oven, generally for cooking food. By moving heated air past the food, convection ovens operate at a lower temperature than a standard conventional oven and they can cook food more quickly. They are mostly used in industrial and commercial applications, but can be purchased for the home as well. With a convection oven there will be about a 25 to 30% decrease in cooking temperature and a 20% decrease in cooking time as compared to a conventional oven.

Convection ovens are highly versatile units. They're ideal for cooking, warming, roasting, re-thermalising and baking. Whether you're roasting a turkey or baking croissants, convection ovens cook evenly and thoroughly. Convection ovens are available in gas or electric and in various configurations, including full-size, half-size, stackable, and as part of a traditional bake oven. Convection ovens are highly versatile and ideal for cooking, warming, roasting, re-thermalising and baking. Convection ovens work by forcing heated air, via fans located in the back of the oven wall, over and around the food racks. By moving heated air around the food product, convection ovens do the same job as a rotary oven in a lot less time and using a lot less space. Convection ovens operate at lower temperatures than standard conventional ovens and they cook faster, saving an operator both time and energy. In a convection oven, product that is placed with little space between pans will still cook evenly. Convection ovens offer the operator more flexibility to cook, bake, or steam inject.

Convection cooking reduces product shrinkage and, in some cases, can result in an extra serving. You can use a convection oven to bake and roast anything from meats to pizza, pastries, and crusty breads. One can bake delicate pies and pastries in a convection oven. When these ovens first came on the market, the moving air would create uneven meringues and custards. Today, with the "gentle bake" and diffused air circulation, uneven cooking is no longer a concern. Although both of these ovens use convection to carry heat, only one of them has the word "convection" in its name. The difference between them is that while a standard oven waits for natural convection to move heat slowly from the heat source to the food, a convection oven uses a fan to drive heat rapidly from source to food. While natural may sound appealing, a convection oven is simply better than a standard oven.

Dutch Oven

A Dutch oven is a thick-walled metal cooking pot with a tight-fitting lid. A camping, cowboy or chuck wagon Dutch oven has three legs and a flat, rimmed lid, so that coals from the cooking fire can be placed on top as well as below. This provides more uniform internal heat and lets the inside act as an oven. They are ordinarily made of cast iron, although some are aluminum.

Modern dutch ovens consist of a covered, shallow cooking pan set on legs and heated from below with a built-in electrical heating element. The dutch oven is also a slang name for a practical joke played on bedmates by restraining them under the covers after you have passed gas. Also refers to slang term used to describe the smoking of cannabis or marijuana in a sealed enviroment such as a small room or car for the purpose of inhaling the residual smoke long after the smoking implement has been emptied, thus providing a further high. This is also known as hot-boxing, clam-baking, or fish-bowling.

Cooking techniques such as roasting, baking simmering, stewing, frying, boiling, steaming, and many others are easily done on the campfire with only a single utensil, the dutch oven. Think of the possibilities, delicious fresh baked bread that will rise up and lift the lid, cobblers made from berries picked fresh at the campsite, incredible deep-dish pizzas, stews, quiches that melt in your mouth, cornish game hens roasted to perfection, and imagine a chocolate cake a foot in diameter. These and many, many more are very possible and sometimes easier than they are at home.

Cookware

Cookware comprises cooking vessels, such as saucepans and fry pans, intended for use on a stove or range cooktop. Bakeware comprises cooking vessels intended for use inside an oven. The terms cookware and bakeware are not exclusive, and it is possible for a single utensil to be used as both cookware and bakeware. Knowledge of cooking vessels before the development of pottery is minimal due to the limited archaeological evidence. It has been possible to extrapolate likely developments based on methods used by latter peoples. Among the first of the techniques believed to be used by stone age civilizations were improvements to basic roasting. In addition to exposing food to direct heat from either an open fire or hot embers it is possible to cover the food with mud or large leaves before roasting to preserve moisture in the cooked result. Examples of similar techniques are still in use in many modern cuisines. Of greater difficulty was finding a method to boil water. For people without access to natural heated water sources, such as hot springs, it was possible to prepare a small pit lined with stones and filled with water.

Types of Cookware

Cookware consists of different types of pots and pans that are used for specific purposes. Some of the pieces of cookware can be substituted for a type you may not have and still accomplish the type of cooking you need to perform. Pots and pans are available in different sizes and made of different types of material. Some materials are better than others when used for specific cooking methods. When selecting the cookware for your kitchen, you should take the following points into consideration:

— *Budget*: How much can you afford to spend on the pots and pans you purchase? You should purchase the best quality that you can afford. It will be well worth it in the long run. Otherwise, you will find yourself replacing them in a short time.

— *Cooking Habits*: How much will you be cooking? Do you eat out a lot and buy convenience food or do you like to prepare meals from scratch? Will you be entertaining a lot?

— *Cuisine*: Will you be making a lot of pasta, soups, or stir-fries? There are special pots and pans that assist in preparing these types of food.

— *Quantity*: Will you be cooking for 1, 2 or several? Having the right size cookware will be important when preparing your food.

Cookware is made from many different materials. Understanding the differences will assist you in making the best choice for your needs.

Lined copper: Copper is one of the more expensive materials used to make pots and pans. It conducts heat evenly and is very responsive to heat. It heats up quickly and will also cool down quickly when removed from the heat, preventing sautés and delicate foods from burning and becoming overdone. Because copper distributes heat so evenly and efficiently, it is the best choice for frying and sautéing, but it is also a good choice for many other cooking methods. One problem with copper is that it interacts with everything it comes in contact with. Moisture in the air causes it to form a film on it that is poisonous and salty food causes a chemical reaction that can make food have a metallic taste.

Stainless steel: Stainless steel cookware is moderately priced. It is the most versatile material to use because it keeps its bright shine and has good tensile strength, preventing it from denting easily. Stainless steel is a good material for any type of pan because it does not corrode and does not react with alkaline or acidic materials. The one problem with stainless steel is that it does not conduct heat well. To combat this problem, pots and pans made from stainless steel have should have a thick aluminum or copper core in the bottom of the pan to help conduct heat more evenly and make the pan more responsive to heat. In the better quality pans, the aluminum or copper core also runs up the sides.

You may find a stainless steel pan with an aluminum or copper plate on the bottom but if the plate is not thick enough, it will not do an efficient job of conducting heat evenly. To care for stainless steel cookware, wash with hot soapy water. A nylon scouring pad or nylon scraper can be used to remove stuck on food. There are stainless steel cleaners that can also be used to remove stains and bring a shine back to the cookware.

Aluminum: Aluminum cookware is fairly inexpensive in comparison to cookware made from other materials. Aluminum is lightweight but fairly strong. It is a good conductor of heat and does not easily distort when exposed to high temperatures. Aluminum works well for sautéing and frying foods because if its heat responsiveness. The drawback of aluminum is that it reacts to acidic and alkaline foods, causing it to corrode and affect the taste of the food being cook. Aluminum is generally used as a core heat conductor, or coated with stainless steel or an anodised coating to protect the food. To care for aluminum cookware, wash the pans with hot soapy water. Avoid washing the cookware in hard water because it tends to darken the aluminum. To remove stains, use a cream of tarter and water paste.

Anodized aluminum: This is aluminum that has been given a special finish to protect it from corrosion. It is a good conductor of heat and the special finish makes it stick-resistant. It is a good choice of material to look for in pots and pans for most any type of cooking. Pots and pans made from anodized aluminum are not dishwasher safe and can be dark in colour, making it hard to see slight colour changes in the food being cooked. To care for anodized aluminum pans, do not cook foods that are highly acidic or alkaline in them because they have a tendency to cause pitting in the coating. They should be washed by hand in hot soapy water rather than in a dishwasher where the strong detergent would damage the surface of the cookware. To avoid scratching the finish, do not use abrasive materials on the surface of anodized aluminum cookware.

Cast iron: Cast iron cookware is inexpensive to moderately priced. It is fairly heavy and conducts heat evenly. It heats slowly but once it is hot it holds the heat well. This makes it good for deep frying and slow-cooking. It can be used on top of the stove and in the oven. Drawbacks to cast iron are that it rusts, stains and becomes pitted when exposed to air, moisture and certain foods. To care for cast iron cookware, do not wash in soapy water but try wiping clean with a paper towel. Run hot water over stuck on food to help loosen and remove. After your cast iron pot has been washed it should be dried thoroughly. To prevent the pan from rusting, rid it of any excess moisture by setting it on the stove over high heat until all moisture has evaporated and coat with oil before storing.

Non-stick: These pots and pans have had a coating applied to them that prevents food from sticking and makes clean up easier. The non-stick surface is really an advantage when cooking some foods, such as omelettes, and when reheating sticky foods, such as rice. It also reduces the amount of fat that is normally required when cooking. The non-stick surface is less efficient when using certain cooking methods, such as sautéing, because the coating interferes with the transfer of heat from the underlying pan. To care for non-stick cookware, use hot soapy water and avoid using abrasive pads or powders. If food does stick to the pan, soak in hot water to loosen stuck on food. A nylon scouring pad, nylon scraper, or nonabrasive cleaner can also be used to help remove stuck on food. Do not wash in a dishwasher. Also protect the non-stick surface by only using wooden, plastic, or coated utensils when cooking.

Types of Pots and Pans

There are many types of pots and pans available for different cooking methods. Many of the types can be used for more than one method. Shown below are some of the different types and a brief description of each.

Braiser pan: A round or oval-shaped pan with two stay-cool handles and heavy domed cover. This is a heavyweight pan made of anodized aluminum or stainless steel. Both types of material contain an aluminum or copper core layer in the middle that runs all across the bottom and up the sides, which spreads heat evenly through the pan.

Braising pans

Braising pans can be used on the stovetop and in the oven. It is important that the cooking vessel has a tight fitting lid so that the liquid does not evaporate. They are available in depths ranging from 2 to 3 inches and in various sizes ranging from 10 to 13 inches in diameter or 2 ½ quarts to 6 quarts. This pan could also be used as a casserole pan.

Casserole: A round or oval pan with steep sides, which ranges in size from 2 quarts to 12 quarts. The casserole pan can be found made from many different materials. It is available made from the same high quality materials as a saucepan or you may find it made from glass, ceramic or earthenware. It may have a cover but many times the cover is not used when cooking the food in a casserole.

Casserole pan

Depending on the material it is made from, it may be used on the stove top but is generally used in the oven. It is used for cooking one-dish meals and the meal is served at the table in the casserole pan.

Chef's pan: A medium depth pan that generally has flared or rounded sides but is sometimes found with straight sides. It has a flat bottom and wide mouth, which accelerates the evaporation of liquids. A chef's pan most often will have a long handle and a tight fitting cover. It is made of a metal with a thick ground base that allows temperature changes to occur rapidly as the level of the heat applied to it changes, either increasing or decreasing for the best heat conduction.

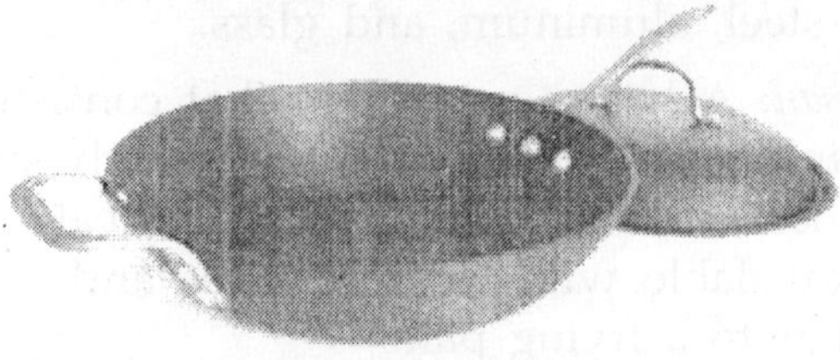

Chef's pan

Chef's pans are available in a variety of sizes such as 2, 3, 4, 5, or 6 quart. The height of the sides make it easier for sautéing, frying or steaming greater amounts of foods, allowing sufficient space for turning and stirring of the contents. Chef's pans are very similar to saucier pans and either pan can be used interchangeably.

Double boiler: A double boiler consists of two pans where one sits inside of the other. The bottom pan is slightly larger so the top pan can fit inside. The bottom pan contains hot water and the top pan holds the ingredients that are being cooked. This type of pan is used when making delicate sauces that have a tendency to separate if cooked on direct heat.

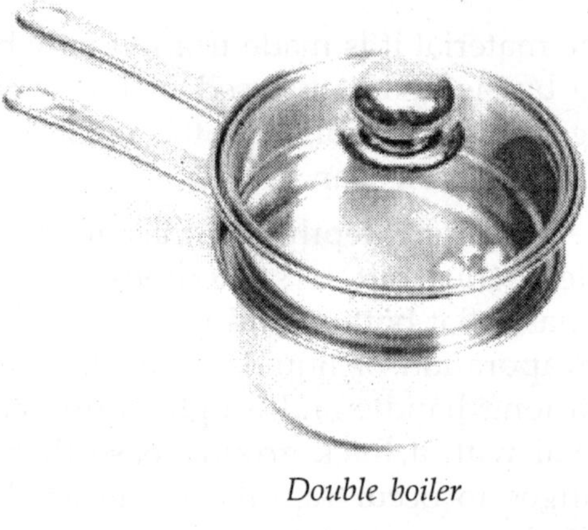

Double boiler

Double boiler are often made from stainless steel but can also be found made from other materials, such as enamelled steel, aluminum, and glass.

Grill pan: A heavy metal pan that consists of ridges spaced evenly across the bottom that closely simulate the grilling process when cooking various meats and foods. They are available with shallow sides and with deeper sides similiar to a frying pan.

Omelette pan: An omelette pan is basically the same as a frying pan. It is available made from the same type of material as frying pans and is generally shaped the same. An omelette pan with a non-stick surface is beneficial when making omelettes because it allows the eggs to release from the pan, making them easier to turn or flip. The omelette pan is also available in an oval shaped pan that is generally 10 to 12 inches long. The oval pan works well for cooking foods such as omelettes, fish filets, and shell steaks. The most common sizes for round pans are 8, 10, and 12 inches.

Roasting pan: A rectangular shaped pan with low sides, which allows the heat from the oven to expose the entire surface of the meat to create a browned exterior. The pan is generally used with a rack to prevent the meat from sitting in its own juices and stewing instead of browning. There are several sizes available. Select a size that allows approximately 2 inches between the side of the pan and the meat. Also, be sure that there is at least 2 inches of space between the outside of the pan and the sides of the oven so that there will be proper air circulation.

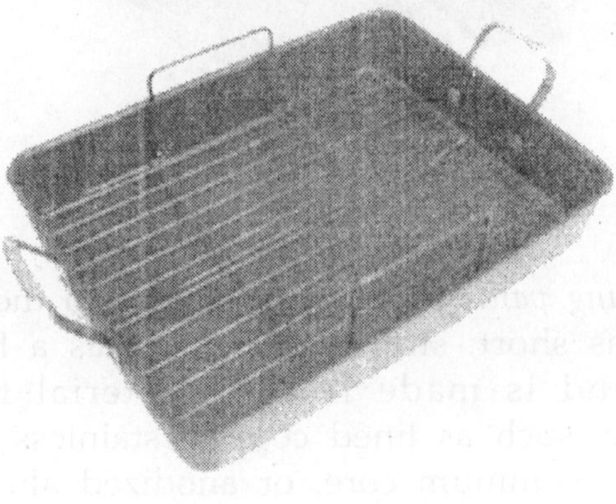

Roasting pan

The roasting pans are available made from several different materials, such as stainless steel, stainless steel with an aluminum or copper core, aluminum with non-stick surfaces, anodized aluminum, lined copper and granite. An oval shaped pan with deep sides and a large domed cover. It generally has a flat rack included on the bottom of the pan. They are available in several sizes and material, such as granite, anodized aluminum, and stainless steel. The meat is cooked with the cover on, which acts as an oven in an oven, resulting in the meat cooking more quickly and in a moister environment. This results in moist, tender meat. The deep-sided roasting pan, generally without the cover, is also used for casseroles.

Saucepan: A round pot with high straight sides and a flat bottom that is used for several purposes, such as cooking vegetables, heating soup, and making sauces. The standard saucepan has straight sides but there are other styles available that are used for special purposes.

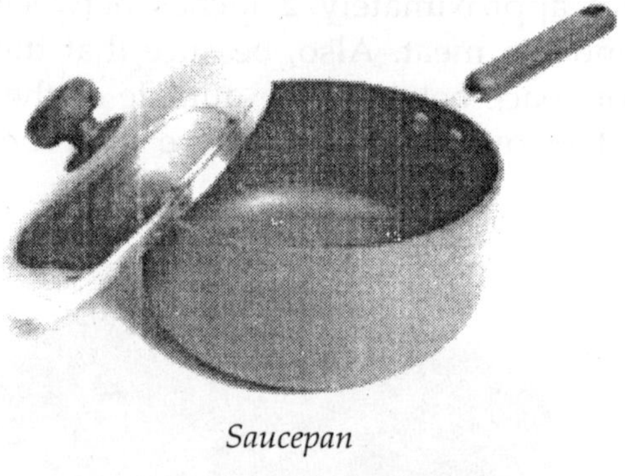

Saucepan

Sauteing pan: A pan very similar to the frying pan, only it has short, straight sides. It has a heavy gauge bottom and is made from a material that is heat responsive, such as lined copper, stainless steel with a copper or aluminum core, or anodized aluminum. It is used for sautéing foods but can also be used for frying foods. The pan should have a long handle and it generally comes with a cover. Some of the larger models have a loop handle opposite the long handle that is used to assist in lifting the pan.

Sauteuse pan: An round, lidded pan with small handles that is often used to sauté or braise a variety of foods. With short to medium height outward sloping sides, a sauteuse pan is a utensil for cooking casseroles, stews, and pasta dishes as well as meat and poultry dishes. Common in European households, this pan has a small curved handle on each side instead of a single straight handle and is typically available in sizes ranging from 2.5 quarts to 7 quarts.

Stir-Fry pan: A round, deep pan that may have straight sides with a slightly rounded base or more commonly a round base that slopes out and upward. Stir fry pans are available with several different sized handle lengths that can be selected to match the cooking process. The pan allows heat to be well distributed across the base while the sloping sides make it easier to stir and turn ingredients as they cook. The Asian pan referred to as a "wok" is one traditional type of stir-fry pan while other versions are often available with bases and sides that are thicker in substance, not as curved, nor as deep as the wok pan. Stir fry pans are often used to prepare and quickly sear multiple ingredients that go well together including various meats and vegetables mixed with sauces. The stir fry pan is good for cooking food in a small quantity of oil and for retaining the colours and textures of the various ingredients.

Stockpot: A deep, straight-sided pot that is taller than it is wide. It has two, securely attached, loop handles that are big enough to easily allow the use of potholders or oven mitts. It is used for simmering large amount of liquid, such as stock, soup and stews, but also works well for thick soups, chilli and for boiling pasta. The pot does not need to be made of anodized aluminum or copper to promote responsive heat reaction but should have a heavy bottom to protect against burning and scorching. Stockpots are available in sizes ranging from 6 quarts to 20 quarts and generally include a cover. 10, 12 and 14 quarts are standard sizes that will satisfy many uses. You will find stockpots made of several different materials, such as stainless steel, aluminum, anodized aluminum, copper, and non-stick materials.

Wok: A bowl shaped pan that is used to quickly cook food over high heat. It is available with a rounded or flat bottom. The traditional type wok has a rounded bottom and is used over a flamed heat source, such as a gas burner. The flat bottom wok was designed to use on an electric burner or a ceramic stovetop but can also be used on a gas stove.

The rounded woks come with a ring that should be placed over the flames to hold the woks steady. Woks are available made from various materials, such as carbon steel, cast iron, stainless steal with aluminum inner layers, and metal with a non-stick coating applied. Cast steel and cast iron woks must be seasoned before they are used for the first time. Some varieties of woks have one long handle, some have two short handles and others have a long handle on one side and a short one on the opposite side.

Bakeware

There are many different types of bakeware, such as, round pans, square pans, rectangle pans, tube pans, bundt pans, jelly roll pans, loaf pans, springform pans, roasting pans, and casseroles. Your recipe will suggest that you use a certain size and type of pan. If you do not have the pan requested, you can generally substitute a similar size pan without any problem. The information below will help you make the appropriate substitution. Select a pan that is as close to the same size as the pan the recipe indicated to use. The pan should have approximately the same volume capacity and when filled, the ingredients should be close to the same depth as they would be in the original size pan.

Food Processing Equipments

Food processing takes clean, havested or slaughtered and butchered components and uses these to produce attractive and marketable food products. Similar process are used to produce animal feed. A food processor is a kitchen appliance used to facilitate various repetitive tasks in the process of preparation of food. It helps to chop, slice, shred, grind, and puree almost any food quickly and easily. Some models can also assist the home cook in making citrus and vegetable juice, beating cake batter, kneading bread dough, beating egg whites, and grinding meats and vegetables.

Today, the term almost always refers to an electric-motor-driven appliance, although there are some manual devices also referred to as "food processors". Food processors are similar to blenders in many ways. The primary difference is that food processors use swappable blades and disks (attachments) instead of a fixed blade. Also, their bowls are wider and shorter, a more appropriate shape for the solid or semi-solid foods usually worked in a food processor.

Its functions normally consist of:

— Slicing/chopping vegetables

— Grinding items such as nuts, meat, or dried fruit

— Shredding or Grating cheese or vegetables

— Pureeing

— Mixing and kneading doughs

Modern food processors come in three basic sizes: full, compact, and mini. No matter what size they are, however, the basic components are the same: a motor, a bowl with a lid and feed tube, and a set of attachments. The motor is housed in the base of the appliance, and it is the heaviest part of the device. Full-size machines generally have larger, more powerful motors, and can weigh more than 20 lbs (9 kg). This weight has a utilitarian value: The heaviness of the base gives the appliance stability and ensures that it doesn't move around while the motor is running.

Though the first food processor bases were clad only in white, hard plastic, today they are available in a range of stylish colours and with metal and plastic finishes, ensuring that your appliance will fit in with your kitchen decor. From the motor, a shaft extends upward to power the attachments. The bowl, which is usually made of durable, transparent plastic, fits onto this shaft and locks into position. The lid, usually made of the same material, locks onto the top of the bowl; in many older models, engaging the locking mechanism turns on the motor, but newer models generally have an on/off switch or button.

Mixers

A mixer is a kitchen appliance intended for mixing, folding, beating, and whipping food ingredients. Mixers come in two major variations, hand mixers and stand mixers. A hand mixer, as the name implies, is a hand-held device. It typically consists of a handle mounted over a large enclosure containing the motor, which drives two beaters. The beaters are immersed in the food to be mixed. Hand mixers are often battery-powered.

Blenders

A blender is a kitchen appliance used to blend ingredients or puree food. The term typically refers to a stationary, upright electrical device, which is to be distinguished from a hand-powered or electric mixer that may be used for similar purposes.

A typical blender is built around a vessel for the ingredients to be blended. At the top of the vessel is a cap to prevent ingredients from escaping when the blender is switched on. At the bottom is a blade assembly, typically removable for cleaning purposes. The bottom seal is most likely watertight. The vessel rests upon a base containing a motor (for turning the blade assembly) with controls on its surface. Most modern blenders offer a number of possible speeds.

Coffee Makers

Most people who are dependent on caffeine have breakfast with an old friend — the coffee maker! Every morning you scoop in the coffee, add the water and turn it on, but have you ever wondered what is happening inside? How does the water get from the little compartment where you pour it in to the top of the coffee maker, and what is that gurgling sound?

A modern drip coffee maker is a surprisingly simple device. Manufacturers have had 25 years to hone their designs, so these coffee makers are pretty straightforward once you open them up.

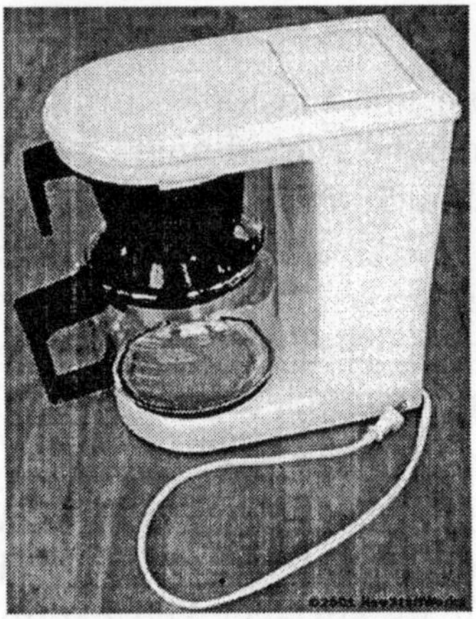

Coffee Maker

If you take off the top of the coffee maker, you find three things:

— There is a little bucket that holds the water when you pour it into the pot at the start of the coffee-making cycle (on the right in the picture above). There is a hole in the bottom of the bucket, and its role will become obvious in a moment.

— There is a black tube that carries the hot water to the drip area.

— There is the drip area (on the left-hand side of this picture). Water arrives here from the black hot-water tube and simply falls through the holes into the coffee grounds.

The heating element is an aluminum extrusion with two parts: a resistive heating element and a tube for water to flow through. The resistive heating element is simply a coiled wire, very similar to the filament of a light bulb or the element in an electric toaster, that gets hot when you run electricity through it. In a resistive element like this, the coil is embedded in a plaster to make it more rugged.

TOASTERS

For lots of people, the toaster is a daily part of breakfast (and lunch and maybe even dinner). A toaster is a machine for toasting food such as sliced bread and bagels. Toasted bread is called toast. Other toastable products may be described as toaster pastry. A typical toaster uses infrared radiation to heat a piece of bread. The heat is usually produced by conducting electricity through nichrome wires (Joule heating).

The toasting process consists of reducing the bread's water content, raising its temperature, and slightly charring and caramelising its surface. The caramelisation process is a chemical reaction in which the complex starch molecules break apart into simpler sugar molecules upon heating. That is why toast is usually sweeter than normal bread.

Toaster

Toaster ovens perform toasting functions of a pop-up toaster, however, the heating elements are positioned horizontally. A toaster oven usually has a glass door and a pull out tray upon which the object to be toasted is placed. Because of its design, a toaster oven can also perform some of the functions provided by a regular oven, but on a somewhat smaller scale. Toaster ovens are freestanding units, commonly placed on countertops or hung from cupboards (kitchen cabinets). It is highly recommended that no one attempts to retrieve toast and other objects from the toaster using silverware such as a knife because of the risk of electric shock.

The most common way for a toaster to create the infrared radiation is to use nichrome wire wrapped back and forth across a mica sheet. Toaster heating element, nichrome wire on mica sheet. Nichrome wire is an alloy of nickel and chromium. It has two features that make it a good producer of heat:

— Nichrome wire has a fairly high electrical resistance compared to something like copper wire, so even a short length of it has enough resistance to get quite hot.

— The nichrome alloy does not oxidise when heated. Iron wire would rust very quickly at the temperatures seen in a toaster.

The very simplest toaster would have two mica sheets wrapped in nichrome wire, and they would be spaced to form a slot about an inch (2.5 cm) wide. The nichrome wires would connect directly to a plug.

Pressure Cookers

A pressure cooker is often used by mountain climbers to compensate for the low atmospheric pressure at a very high altitude. Without it, water boils off before reaching 100 °C, leaving the food improperly cooked, as described in Charles Darwin's *Voyage of the Beagle*: At the place where we slept water necessarily boiled, from the diminished pressure of the atmosphere, at a lower temperature than it does in a less lofty country; the case being the converse of that of a Papin's digester. Hence the potatoes, after remaining for some hours in the boiling water, were nearly as hard as ever. The pot was left on the fire all night, and next morning it was boiled again, but yet the potatoes were not cooked. I found out this, by overhearing my two companions discussing the cause, they had come to the simple conclusion, "that the cursed pot [which was a new one] did not choose to boil potatoes."

A larger scale version of a pressure cooker, used by laboratories and hospitals to sterilise biological waste materials, surgical instruments etc. is known as an autoclave. Pressure cookers create healthier, tastier meals and yet have remained an enigma to American cuisine and cooks. Because food cooks faster at higher temperatures, this cooking utensil works its magic by creating the necessary pressure to increase the temperature without burning the food. For example, water (which at sea level normally boils at 212° Fahrenheit) boils under pressure when the temperature is 30-50° higher than normal. The food cooks thoroughly and evenly, the nutrients stay in the food, and you get risotto in 7 minutes, artichokes in 10 minutes, beef stew in 15 minutes, cheese cake in 30 minutes.

Food properly cooked in a pressure cooker is safer, because it is cooked at higher temperatures that do a better job of killing microorganisms.

Pressure Cooker

New pressure cookers, with their multiple safety features and improved vent systems, are once more catching on in The United States. These vessels offer a choice of a quick-release option, taking even less time to finish that meal and without the need for the water to cool down. Busy cooks with hectic schedules, demanding jobs, an active family and little spare time are looking for fast, economical ways for preparing home-cooked, nutritious meals. Television ads market overpriced cookers with fancy new names, touting the "latest, greatest new invention" to cooks who would never have considered buying a pressure cooker. Wide spread advertising has brought with it a resurgence of interest in pressure cookery, and now this old fashioned cooking method is suddenly new again!

The moral of the story is a moot one indeed. If you get a used pressure cooker, it is crucial to make sure that the gaskets (rubber seals) are still in the top of the pressure cooker. You must also make sure that the steam vent works properly. If you opt to buy a new cooker, keep in mind that the 6-quart size is the standard for most recipes. Select a cooker with a detachable pressure regulator that can adjust the pressure to low, medium and high. The higher the pressure, the higher the internal temperature and the less cooking time required. The safety valve automatically vents steam. Choose a pot with heat resistant handles, a locking lid that is easy to manoeuvre and a heavy bottom of stainless steel construction so that the same pot can be used to do preparatory sauteing.

Rice cooker: A rice cooker or rice steamer is a self-contained electrical appliance, used primarily for cooking rice. There are also microwave, gas and open flame variants. The preparation of rice has traditionally been a tricky cooking process that requires accurate timing, and errors can result in inedible undercooked or burnt rice. Rice cookers aim to avoid these problems by automatically controlling the heat and timing in the preparation of the rice, while at the same time freeing up a heating element on the range. Although the rice cooker does not necessarily speed the cooking process, the cook's involvement in cooking rice with a rice cooker is significantly reduced and simplified.

Typically, a rice cooker contains an insulated outer container containing a heating element, into which is fitted a non-stick or teflon-coated inner removable bowl, which often has graduations marked in cups of rice (white). Whereas less expensive and older models use simple electronics and mechanical and thermal sensors, high-end rice cookers use microchips to control the cooking process and often incorporate a timer which can be used to set the desired "ready time". Many rice cookers can keep rice warm safely for up to 24 hours. This helps to avoid the dangers of food poisoning due to Bacillus cereus. Rice cookers, when purchased, normally include a small "cup" measure and a plastic paddle for doling out the cooked rice.

Restaurants that serve a lot of rice, particularly those specialising in Asian cuisine, often use industrial size rice cookers that quickly and cheaply produce large quantities of cooked rice. A rice cooker is a standard appliance in kitchens around the world, especially in Asian countries. The bowl in the rice cooker is usually removable, and beneath it lies a spring and thermostat. These form the main components of the rice cooker. The spring in the bottom is simply to ensure contact of the thermostat to the base of the cooking bowl.

In a rice cooker the amount of rice and water are exactly measured. During cooking the mixture is continuously heated. The temperature cannot go above the boiling point of water—100°C (212°F)—as any energy put into the system at that point will only cause the water to boil. At the end of cooking all of the water will have been evaporated or absorbed by the rice. If the heating continues past this point the temperature surpasses the boiling point. The thermostat then trips, and switches the rice cooker to "warm" mode, keeping the rice no cooler than approximately 65°C (150°F) (simple rice cookers, like the one below, may simply turn off at this point).

To cook white rice, the rice is measured and optionally rinsed, then added to the inner bowl. Cold water is measured and added or simply added up to the appropriate graduation in the inner bowl. Sometimes there are separate scales for brown rice or for cooking other foods in the appliance. Once the lid is closed and the cooking cycle has been activated, the rice cooker does the rest. Fancy models give a countdown in minutes to the "ready time," and beep when done, whereas less expensive and older models simply click or ring a bell when done.

Rice cookers are typically used for the preparation of plain or lightly seasoned rice, but more elaborate recipes are possible using a rice cooker, and there are cookbooks devoted entirely to dishes prepared using a rice cooker. One of the more unexpected dishes that can be made in a rice cooker is a beef stew. By simply adding ingredients and setting it to "warm", a rice cooker would cook that at about 65°C (150°F). In few hours, the stew is fully cooked and ready to eat.

Some rice cookers are designed to accommodate a basket above the rice. This basket is generally used to steam vegetables, holding them in the steam coming off the rice. Some vegan cooks consider rice cookers to be an invaluable tool in the preparation of vegan meals. They find it extremely versatile, allowing a variety of meals to be cooked with minimal preparation and no attention during the cooking process, which suits contemporary busy lifestyles well.

REFRIGERATORS

Refrigeration and freezing are used on almost all foods: meats, fruits, vegetables, beverages, etc. In general, refrigeration has no effect on a food's taste or texture. Freezing has no effect on the taste or texture of most meats, has minimal effects on vegetables, but often completely changes fruits (which become mushy). Refrigeration's minimal effects account for its wide popularity. The fundamental reason for having a refrigerator is to keep food cold. Cold temperatures help food stay fresh longer.

The basic idea behind refrigeration is to slow down the activity of bacteria (which all food contains) so that it takes longer for the bacteria to spoil the food. For example, bacteria will spoil milk in two or three hours if the milk is left out on the kitchen counter at room temperature. However, by reducing the temperature of the milk, it will stay fresh for a week or two — the cold temperature inside the refrigerator decreases the activity of the bacteria that much. By freezing the milk you can stop the bacteria altogether, and the milk can last for months.

Refrigeration and freezing are two of the most common forms of food preservation used today. There are many options to choose from when shopping for a new refrigerator. Choices include a variety of models and styles that have new convenience and energy-saving features. Before purchasing a refrigerator, it is a good idea to measure the space available for the new refrigerator as well as door and hallway clearances. These measurements can be compared to the refrigerator's outside dimensions to make sure it will fit into the kitchen. When deciding what size of refrigerator to purchase, a rule-of-thumb is a minimum of 12 cubic feet for the first two persons in the household, plus 2 more cubic feet for each additional person.

A refrigerator (often shortened to fridge) or freezer is an electrical appliance that uses refrigeration to help preserve food. A domestic refrigerator is present in 99.5% of American homes. It works using phase change heat pumps operating in a refrigeration cycle. An industrial refrigerator or industrial freezer is simply a refrigerator used in an industrial setting, usually in a restaurant or supermarket. They may consist of either a cooling compartment only (a larger refrigerator) or a freezing compartment only (a freezer) or contain both.

Types of Refrigerator

Side-by-side Refrigerators

The newest *side-by-side refrigerators* are the three-door models. Some have upper freezers that allow easy access to frequently used items with a minimal loss of cold air as well as lower freezers for long-term frozen food storage. For families that require a lot of refrigerator space, there are the separate refrigerator and freezer units designed to be used together. These units can be as large as 30 cubic feet each.

Built-in Refrigerators

Built-in refrigerators and freezers are made to be flush with surrounding cabinets. To create the built-in look, custom panels can be placed on doors to match cabinets. Unlike top-mounted refrigerator/freezer models, which are about 30 inches deep, built-ins are only 24 inches deep. Some of the built-in refrigerator/freezers are taller, as much as 19 inches higher than top-mounted refrigerator/freezers, and they are 5 inches wider.

Pull-down Door or Access Door Models

Pull-down door or access door models have small doors in the refrigerator that allow access to shelves inside the refrigerator. Frequently used items can be stored on those shelves and energy can be saved by opening only the small doors rather than the full refrigerator doors.

Defrost Systems

With manual-defrost systems, the removal of frost and condensation from both the fresh food and freezer compartments are entirely manual. In partial automatic or cycle defrost systems, only the fresh food compartment is defrosted automatically. The freezer compartment must be emptied and manually defrosted. In automatic or no-frost systems, frost is removed automatically in both the refrigerator and freezer compartments.

Many of the new refrigerators have automatic ice makers. These are either factoryinstalled or available as an optional kit for later installation. Automatic ice makers increase energy costs by as much as 300 kwh per year, or about $21 a year at .07 cents per kwh. The refrigerator must be plumbed to a water line, which is an additional installation cost. Adjustable food storage controls allow the consumer to change the temperature and/or humidity of the different compartments for such foods as fresh vegetables, fruits, puddings, meats, and cheeses. An energy saver switch located inside the refrigerator can be shut off when humidity is low, thus saving energy.

Gas Absorption Refrigerator

The absorption refrigerator is a refrigerator that utilizes a heat source to provide the energy needed to drive the cooling system rather than being dependent on electricity to run a compressor. These refrigerators are popular where electricity is unreliable, costly, or unavailable.

In the developing world gas absorption refrigerators running on kerosene are very valuable where there is no reliable electricity supply. Besides the obvious advantages for food preservation, they supply safe storage of vaccines and drugs. In the developed world, including the United States, absorption refrigerators are most often used for camping and in recreational vehicles, though some are used in remote areas or in off grid homes.

The heat source that powers the refrigeration cycle is most often a propane burner, though other fuel gases such as butane and natural gas are sometimes used instead in areas where these are more readily available. Electricity can provide the heat for an absorption refrigerator and many camping versions can be switched to use it. In extremely remote areas, kerosene is used.

The cooling components of absorption refrigerators can be constructed without moving parts and with no reliance on electricity. However, most new units have thermostats, ignition systems, safety pilot controls, and lights that introduce some moving parts and reliance on a nominal amount of electricity — little enough to be supplied by a dry cell or battery. These refrigerators have the disadvantage of using a lethal gas, ammonia, although it is contained within a closed system; and if they are being run using an open flame then attention has to be paid to its safety and to maintaining the flame at an appropriate size.

Gas and Propane Refrigerators

If you own an RV or use a refrigerator where electricity is not available, chances are you have a gas- or propane-powered refrigerator. These refrigerators are interesting because they have no moving parts and use gas or propane as their primary source of energy. Also, they use heat, in the form of burning propane, to produce the cold inside the refrigerator. A gas refrigerator uses ammonia as the coolant, and it uses water, ammonia and hydrogen gas to create a continuous cycle for the ammonia.

Small Ammonia Refrigerator

Anhydrous Ammonia (Nh_3) has been used for many years to perform all types of refrigeration and air conditioning chores. Anhydrous Ammonia means ammonia without water, Aqua Ammonia is a solution of ammonia and water which is used in refrigeration and air conditioners that are not a vapour compression type. Vapor compression systems use compressors to compress the ammonia vapor.

Absorption type systems do not use a compressor but instead use a generator. Ammonia Refrigeration Basics is a good source of basic information should you require a better understanding on the subject.

Dishwashers

In some countries dishwashing is usually done with a brush instead of a sponge. Collect all of your cutlery into a pile. Remove food scraps and stack the plates and bowls neatly. Find all the coffee mugs, wine glasses, and what-have-you, and group them next to the sink. Arrange your dishes so that they are all in easy reach for when you are standing over the sink. Empty all glasses or other containers before filling the sink. In some European countries the dishes are always washed in a separate tub placed inside the sink. This was a matter of hygiene, as the kitchen sink was the only sink available for all the household water. The clothes were washed in the sink; the water used to wash the floor went down the sink, and so it made sense to separate the dishwater from the sink. There were two other possible reasons. Kitchen sinks tended to be very large in a time when heating water was considered to be a major household expense — a tub used less water. Also kitchen sinks were usually made of hard ceramic; any contact between the sink and plates was liable to cause chips, but a tub could be made of more forgiving material.

Using a separate washing-up bowl in the sink also provides a place to dispose of unfinished drink, soaking-water, etc. Washing up gloves may be worn when washing dishes. Also, modern devices which consist of a sponge mounted on a hollow plastic handle may also be used. The handle is filled with soap, which impregnates the sponge and is gradually released as the dishes are washed. This precludes the necessity of filling a sink or tub with soapy water, which eventually gets dirty. In cases where dishes are to be shared among many, such as restaurants, sanitising may be desirable. These are some steps to sanitise dishes.

— Scrape and rinse to remove visible food particles.

— Soak items briefly in soapy warm water, scrub, sponge.

— Rinse in clean water to remove soap.

— Rinse in dilute bleach solution.

— Allow to air dry.

Dishes are placed on large trays and fed onto rollers through the machine. The use of bleach is critical to sanitation when large groups are involved. While toxic to the environment and not to be used more than necessary, it evaporates completely, is cheap, and kills almost everything. Cabinets, refrigerators, countertops and anything else touched by people in a large group setting should be periodically wiped or sprayed with a dilute bleach solution after being washed with soapy water and rinsed in clean water.

Hand dishwashing: Hand dishwashing is probably subject to more variables than any other household clean-up job. In theory at least, any detergent or soap can be used for hand dishwashing, except an automatic dishwasher detergent. However, soap has become almost extinct as a dishwashing product and many laundry detergents are not very acceptable. Laundry detergents, may leave spots and streaks, the powders may not completely dissolve, or may discolour certain metals with soaking. A light-duty liquid hand dishwashing detergent is the best choice. Regardless of brand, certain characteristics are important in a hand dishwashing liquid: lasting suds, effective cleaning performance, mildness to hands, safety for dishes and other washables, storage stability, pleasant fragrance and appearance, convenient packaging and dispensing. In formulating a product to meet these criteria, manufacturers, in general, use certain basic ingredients. Surfactants or surface active agents are the primary ingredients in a liquid hand dishwashing detergent. Often a combination of surfactants is used to produce good grease cutting capability and soil suspension, mildness in water of varying degrees of hardness, and a high, stable suds level. All surfactants in these detergents are biodegradable. Stability and Dispensing Aids are added to keep the product homogeneous under varying storage conditions, and to provide desirable dispensing characteristics.

Alcohols, hydrotropes, and salts are often used. Fragrance and Colour Additives are what give a product its "personality," and are important, though present in extremely small amounts. Mildness Additives may include moisturising agents, certain oils and emollients, certain protein compounds, or other neutralising or beneficial ingredients. Preservatives are added, if needed, in small quantities to help prevent any microbiological growth in the product which could cause colour or odour change, poor performance and separation of the ingredients.

Mechanical dishwasher: The term dishwasher can represent either a person who washes dishes or a machine that performs a similar function. A dishwasher is a mechanical device for cleaning food utensils for preparation, keeping, serving and eating and drinking. They are found in restaurants and also in many kitchens of homes. The dishwasher therefore is mainly a device for spraying water on the dishes—first detergent-added water for cleaning purposes, then clean water to remove the detergent residue. Some dishwashers also contain a heating element to achieve fast drying of the dishes. In today's kitchens, an automatic dishwasher is no longer a luxury. Automatic dishwashers use less water and sanitise dishes far better than hand washing.

6

EQUIPMENT INSTALLATION

Equipment shall not be located under exposed or unprotected sewer lines, open stairwells or other sources of contamination. The following outlines some of the equipment installation requirements to insure proper spacing and sealing to allow for adequate and easy cleaning:

Food equipment shall be installed as follows:

1. Counter-mounted equipment shall be on 4-inch sanitary legs, sealed to the counter or be portable.
2. Floor-mounted equipment shall be on 6-inch sanitary legs, on casters, or sealed to the floor.
3. Equipment not on casters or not portable shall be sealed to the wall and/or adjoining equipment, or spaced to facilitate cleaning.
4. Portable equipment and equipment installed on casters shall be installed with flexible utility lines and/or quick-disconnect couplings.

The above criteria shall be applied to permit all exposed areas of equipment and adjacent surfaces to be accessible for cleaning. If an item of equipment is not portable, is not installed on casters, or is not otherwise easily moved, it shall be

1. sealed to adjoining surfaces with an approved sealant or metal flashing, or
2. provided with sufficient space between and behind the equipment to allow easy access.

Dishwashing Equipment

Install dishwashing equipment and drainboards a minimum of 3 inches from any adjacent wall area. Drainboards may be manufactured with continuous side and back splashes and mounted directly to the adjoining wall area. Backsplashes must adjoin the wall within 1/32 of an inch and be caulked and sealed to create a smooth, sanitary, vermin proof installation. Where equipment does not effectively adjoin the wall within 1/32 of an inch it should be installed a minimum of 3 inches off the wall.

Soiled Drainboards are recommended to be located a minimum of 18" from food contact surfaces or equipped with splash protection. Splashguard protection is required if spacing to adjoining food, food contact surfaces, or utensil washing and storage area surfaces are less than 18 inches. Splashguards shall not hinder access to the lavatory, should extend from the front of the sink to 12 inches above the rim of the sink, and be of easily cleanable construction.

Portable Equipment

Food equipment that is small and light enough to be easily moved by one person shall be considered portable and is exempt from equipment installation requirements. Figure 1 illustrates some examples of portable equipment. The hot plate and toaster are both equipped with an electrical connection that can be disconnected.

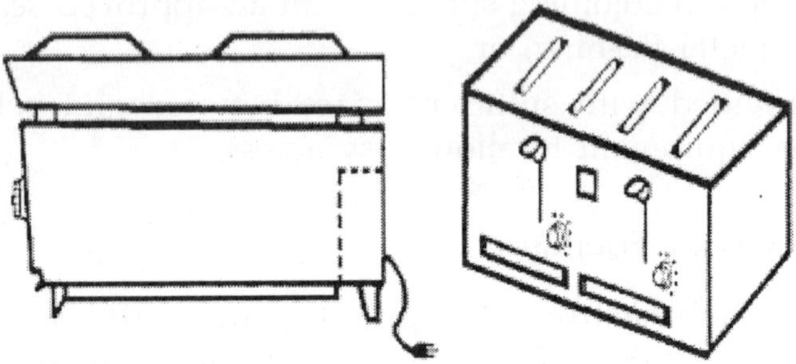

Electric Hot Plate Toaster

Figure 1. Examples of portable equipment

INSTALLATION OF EQUIPMENT

Food equipment, which is not readily movable because of size, weight, or rigid utility connections, shall be installed on counters or tables as follows:

1. On 4-inch sanitary legs; or
2. Sealed to the counter; and
3. Properly spaced to facilitate cleaning; or
4. Equipped with an integral lift lever, pivoting foot, polyethylene wear strips, or a similar device, which allows easy access under and around the equipment for cleaning.

UNDERCOUNTER INSTALLATION

Undercounter equipment installed on the floor shall be equipped with casters or sanitary skids, or on 6-inch sanitary legs and sealed to adjacent surfaces or properly spaced to facilitate cleaning.

CASTERS

Casters shall be properly sized for the equipment served,

and should be compatible with the cleaning materials used. It is strongly recommended that equipment be installed on casters when possible. Equipment installed on casters allows easy movement and facilitates the cleaning of surrounding surfaces and equipment.

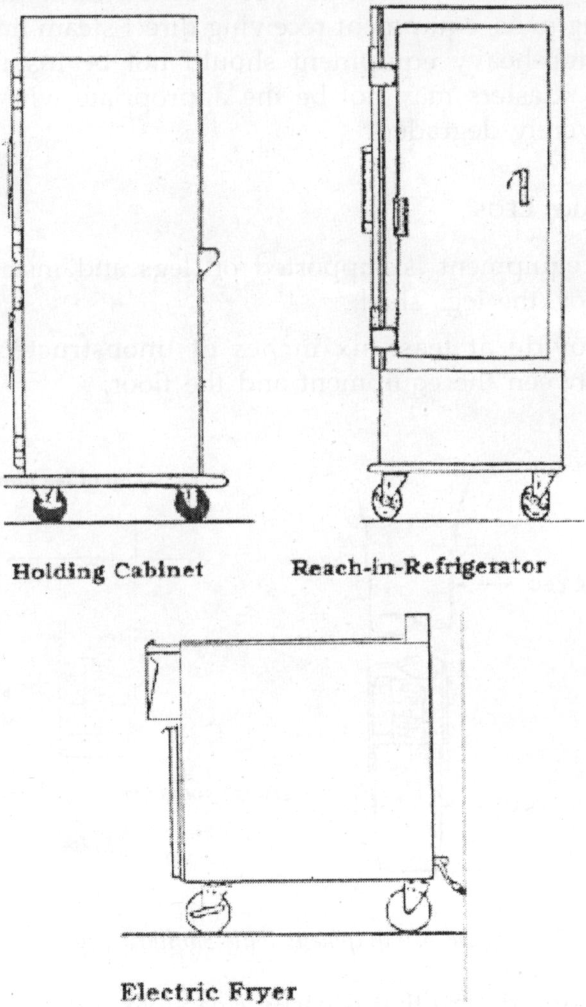

Figure 2. Equipment on casters.

Casters also allow for maximum utilisation of space by reducing or eliminating spacing requirements for cleaning. Casters can be installed on most food equipment, including ice machines and deck ovens. Flexible or quick-disconnect couplings are needed on caster-mounted equipment with utility connections. Due to safety concerns, some tilting braising pans, equipment receiving direct steam lines, and some top-heavy equipment should not be installed on casters. Casters may not be the appropriate when floors are severely degraded.

Sanitary Legs

When equipment is supported on legs and installed on the floor, the legs shall:

1. Provide at least six inches of unobstructed space between the equipment and the floor;

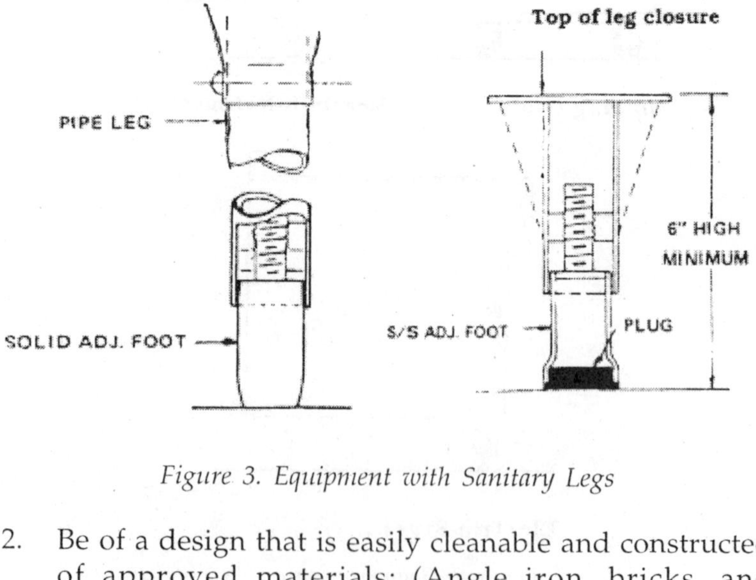

Figure 3. Equipment with Sanitary Legs

2. Be of a design that is easily cleanable and constructed of approved materials; (Angle iron, bricks, and concrete blocks are not approved)

3. Be arranged and built to prevent internal harborage of vermin or accumulation of liquids and debris;
4. Provide a minimum of interference with cleaning at the leg-floor contact,
5. Contain no exposed threads, or embellishments, or overhanging edges that serve as places for accumulation of dust, dirt, and debris.

Island Installation of Equipment

Island installation of equipment reduces the total floor area that must be cleaned. Masonry islands should be a minimum height of six inches with a cove of at least 1/4" inch radius at the juncture of the island and the floor. The edges of the equipment should overhang the island (but not more than the height of the island) to prevent grease or other liquids which may spill over or run down the sides from running underneath. The juncture between the base of the equipment and the island shall be sealed to prevent vermin harborage. Remember to plan for a of 30 inches minimum and 36 inches preferred for a single aisle, 48 inches minimum and 60 inches preferred for a double aisle.

Spacing Requirements

Equipment not readily movable or sealed to adjacent surfaces shall be spaced to allow access for cleaning. The amount of space required between and behind equipment depends on the size of the equipment and the accessibility needed for cleaning the equipment and adjacent surfaces.

1. Provided access is available from both ends of the equipment and the total equipment length is four feet or less (A), the equipment shall be spaced at least six inches from walls and other equipment (B).

2. Provided access is available from both ends of the equipment and the total equipment length is over four feet but less than eight feet (A), the equipment shall be spaced at least 12 inches from walls and other equipment (B).

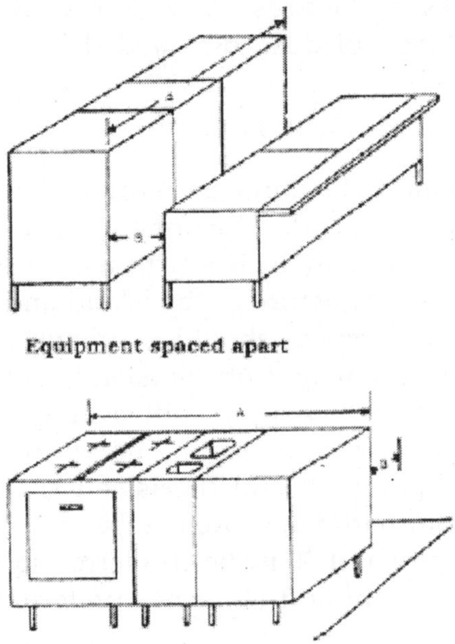

Equipment spaced apart

Equipment sealed together

Figure 4. Installation of minimum space requirements for food

3. When the total equipment length is eight feet or more (A), the equipment shall be spaced at least 18 inches from walls and other equipment (B).
4. A minimum of six inches of space shall be provided between items of equipment to allow access for cleaning. Additional space may be required for large equipment when six inches is not adequate to provide access.

5. Obstruction of the access opening between and/or behind equipment by a chase or rigid utility connection may require additional spacing.

Floor-mounted Equipment

Equipment placed directly on the floor, such as counters, display cases, cabinets, proofers, ovens, large cooking kettles and retarders shall be effectively sealed to the floor using silicone, metal flashing, vinyl coved base, or other approved material.

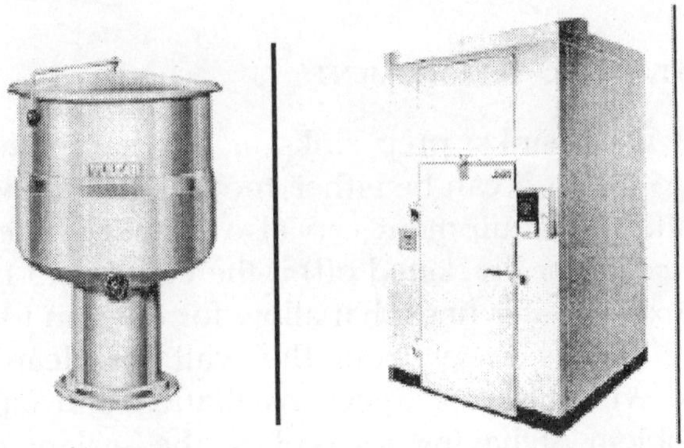

Cooking Kettle **Bakers Oven**

Figure 5. Floor-mounted equipment

Metal kick plates which are readily removable will not be required to be sealed to the floor, provided the base of the equipment is sealed to the floor or the areas behind the kick plates are easily cleanable.

Wall Attached Equipment

Equipment attached to walls, such as lavatories, preparation sinks, utensil washing sinks, dish tables, counters, and cabinets shall be effectively sealed to the wall to prevent splash, debris accumulation, and vermin harborage. Any combination of low profile or pan head bolts, screws, rivets, silicone sealers, or flashing that effectively closes the opening between the equipment and the walls in a smooth and sanitary manner is acceptable. If the equipment is open underneath, such as a drainboard, dish table, or open base table, it may be installed at least three inches away from the wall. This provision is made due to the fact that dish tables, drainboards, and immobile open base tables are accessible underneath the counter top and a space of three inches from the wall to the equipment is enough to facilitate cleaning.

Free Standing Attachment

Utensil wash sinks, prep sinks or any sink that requires water to the unit can be either mounted to the wall or off the wall. The equipment can also installed free standing (not attached or bracketed off) if the equipment is installed with flexible water lines that allow for the unit to be pulled 6 to 12 inches away from the wall for cleaning. This method will allow for easier installation and will prevent the problem of having to replace the sealant on a wall attached unit approximately every year. In cases where the space between the equipment and the wall is too large for use of a silicone sealant, metal or other approved flashing is necessary for an effective seal.

Examples of equipment that frequently require metal flashing are walk-in coolers and freezers, retarders, proofers, and large ovens. Some installations may require a combination of flashing and silicone sealant. Equipment mounted on legs and placed against walls and which can be readily moved for cleaning will not be required to be sealed to adjacent surfaces (i.e. work tables and some equipment tables).

Utility Service Lines

Utility service lines and pipes shall not be unnecessarily exposed on walls or ceilings, in walk-in refrigeration units, food preparation areas, equipment washing areas, utensil washing areas, toilet rooms, and vestibules. Exposed utility service lines and pipes shall be installed in a way that does not obstruct or prevent cleaning of the floors, walls, and ceilings. Installation of exposed horizontal utility lines and pipes on the floor is prohibited. Installation of exposed utility line and pipes for service to equipment up to point of attachment should be 6 inches above the floor and 1 inch off the wall.

All utility and service lines and openings through the floor must be sealed adequately. Exposed vertical and horizontal pipes and lines must be kept to a minimum. The installation of exposed horizontal utility lines and pipes on the floor is prohibited. Any insulation material used on utility pipes or lines in the food preparation or dishwashing area must be smooth non-absorbent and easy to clean.

Installation of Sneeze Guard

1. Sneeze Guards (food Shields): Display of unpackaged foods shall be effectively shielded to intercept the direct line between the customer's mouth and the display of food, and shall be designed to minimise contamination by the customer.
2. Shields shall be mounted to intercept a direct line between the customer's mouth and the food display area at the customer-use-position. The vertical distance from the average customer's mouth to the floor shall be considered (1.4 m) 4 ft 6 in to (1.5 m) 5 ft. Special consideration must be given to the average customer's mouth height in educational facilities and other special installations.

3. Shields shall be fabricated of easy-to-clean and sanitary material.
4. Edges of glass or other hazardous material shall be trimmed with a smooth protective member or have a safety edge of parent material.
5. Where the ends of equipment are designed to allow for customer self service, or customer view food shields complying with these standards shall be installed.

7

LAYOUT OF FOOD SERVICE FACILITIES

The layout process described in two separate stages that occur at the same time. One stage deals with the arrangement of individual pieces of equipment, work tables, and sinks into a unit which comprise a functional area or a functional department. The term department is sometimes associated with separate rooms, but this is not necessarily the case with food service operations. In essence, the designer is developing an area where related functions will be performed and may include as many or as few functions as deemed appropriate for the project. To illustrate, one particular area may be developed for the functions of dessert preparation, salad preparation, and sandwich preparation, whereas another project may require three separate areas for these functions.

The second stage of the layout process involves arranging the functional areas or departments into the total facility. For example, the receiving, storage, preparation, production, and warewashing areas and the nonproduction areas, such as rest rooms, lounges, and offices, are brought together to form the basic floor plan for the facility. There may be some question as to whether these two stages of layout are done at the same time. Even though the planner may be working on one stage or the other at any given moment, layout decisions must be considered in terms of both stages.

In essence, the layout of the total facility must be considered when laying out the component areas; and in turn, the layout of the component areas must be considered when laying out the total facility. The layout phase of planning is critical because it integrates most of the factors that affect the food service facility when it is operational.

Flow of Variables

The planning of individual workplaces is followed by a logical grouping of several workplaces to develop work centers and departnents. The combining of workplaces including tables, sinks, and equipment is guided by different concepts of flow. The criteria involved may include employee flow, material or product flow, customer flow, or in some cases, combinations of these. For example, the layout of a short-order cooking area to be staffed by one employee is best done by evaluating the employee's movements. This can be done by determining the frequency of movements anticipated between pairs of equipment and then placing the pairs of equipment that involve the greatest frequency of movement next to one another in the equipment arrangement.

This analysis leads to arrangements that will minimise employee movement and leads to increased productivity. In some instances it may be possible to place equipment in the same vertical plane to completely eliminate employee movements. The use of salamanders above a range or a microwave oven above a work table are examples of this concept. Consideration of combined or multipurpose equipment where appropriate is warranted. The planning of a large dishwashing area to include a continuous dishwashing machine and where employees are primarily working in fixed areas such as the scrapping table, loading the dishwasher, or unloading the dishwasher may be guided by evaluating material flow.

In some situations, the flow of two or more variables may be evaluated to determine the best layout. A salad preparation area may require evaluation of both the flow of foods and the movements of employees in order to arrive at the best layout. In most cases, arrangements that minimise the flow of materials are also those that minimise the movements of employees. This is likely when the materials are moved primarily by workers, but may not be the case if mechanical conveyors are used. If there is any doubt, both flows should be evaluated. Regardless of the type of flow selected as the criterion for layout, the following principles can be applied:

— Flow should be along straight-line paths as much as possible.

— The amount of cross flow or cross traffic should be minimised.

— Backtracking should be minimised.

— Bypassing should be minimised.

These principles of flow, whether applied to the movement of materials or of people, can be used for all types of layout problems. The concept of keeping flow in a straight line is the most important because it results in movements over the shortest distance. To utilise this concept, the designer will visualise or chart the flow involved with several different arrangements and select the one that gives the best straightline pattern. Flow analyses for layout problems involving only a few pieces of equipment are easy to do. Layout problems involving numerous pieces of equipment or areas will require more extensive flow analysis.

Some planners find flow diagrams or string charts a helpful tool in evaluating complex flow patterns. With the great variety of materials and activities found in food service operations, the concept of minimising cross traffic is important because it results in layouts that are free of bottlenecks and congestion. This concept is especially pertinent to fast-food operations, which have peak periods of flow. Cross traffic is minimised by the proper location of aisles, passageways, and doors. Some cross traffic can be tolerated if it results in shorter flow patterns.

However, if the cross traffic creates a hazardous situation, it should be eliminated, even at the cost of increased distance of movement. Cross traffic between employees and guests is undesirable and should be eliminated. Backtracking occurs when a material or person moves from one piece of equipment or an area back to the point where the movement originated. The flow is back along the same path that was just traversed. Of course, many of the tasks required in food service operations involve a sequence of movements that make it practically impossible to eliminate all backtracking. Many of the cooking and production tasks are of this nature. In those situations, minimising the amount of backtracking is all that can be done. This involves evaluating several different equipment or space arrangements to find the best one.

Bypassing is the result of a material or person passing one or more pieces of equipment to get to the next piece of equipment required in the sequence of movements. Several different arrangements of the equipment or areas may have to be evaluated to determine which one results in the least amount of bypassing. As with cross traffic, it is impossible to eliminate all bypassing except in the very simplest of layout problems. The ultimate goal of layout is to develop arrangements of equipment and spaces for the food facility that have primarily straight-line flow paths with a minimum of cross traffic, backtracking, and bypassing.

Layout Decisions

Although flow has been identified as the most important criterion of layout, other modifying considerations which may affect some layout decisions should be evaluated before the arrangement is finalised. These include the following items:

— *Efficient use of utilities.* All equipment requiring steam, for example, may be placed together to economise on installation and operating costs.

— *Efficient use of equipment.* Some individual pieces of equipment that will be used in two or more functional areas can be placed in central locations so they are easily accessible.

— Efficient use of skilled labour. This requires arrangements of equipment that will minimise the movements of skilled personnel. This may increase the movements of other employees or increase the movement of materials. The decision may be based on an economic analysis of different arrangements.

— *Safety.* Some layouts based on the concepts of flow alone may result in an arrangement of equipment that is hazardous. Placing a deep-fat fryer next to a sink creates a dangerous situation, and safety should override flow in this case. Other hazardous arrangements may result when high-temperature equipment is placed adjacent to a traffic aisle or near entrances and exits. If another location is not feasible, sufficient guarding and shielding of the equipment is an alternative solution.

— *Efficient use of space.* Building configurations and shapes may require rearrangement of some layouts to make full use of available space.

— *Environmental factors of noise and odor.* Some pieces of equipment or areas may be isolated from flow paths if they are objectionable and cannot be modified to render them environmentally acceptable. Garbage-can washers or incinerators illustrate this situation.

These modifying criteria may result in arrangements that are more expensive than those based on flow alone. They have to be used, however, to achieve many of the objectives of planning that were identified.

ARRANGEMENT OF EQUIPMENT AND WORKPLACES

The arrangement of equipment and workplaces for functional areas is usually in the form of a straight line or in combinations and modifications of straight-line configurations. The basic patterns that may be used include:

Single Straight-line Arrangement

This is the simplest of designs, but it is limited in the number of pieces of equipment or workplaces that can be arranged. The straight-line arrangement may be placed along a wall or take the form of an island.

Ell-shaped Arrangement

This is a modification of the straight-line arrangement to accommodate more equipment and workplaces; it is sometimes used where linear space is limited. The ell-shaped configuration is very suitable for separating two major groups of equipment. One group of equipment would be placed on one leg of the ell, the other group forming the second leg. An ell-shaped arrangement is shown in Fig. 1.

U-shaped Arrangements

The U-shaped configuration is ideal for small areas where

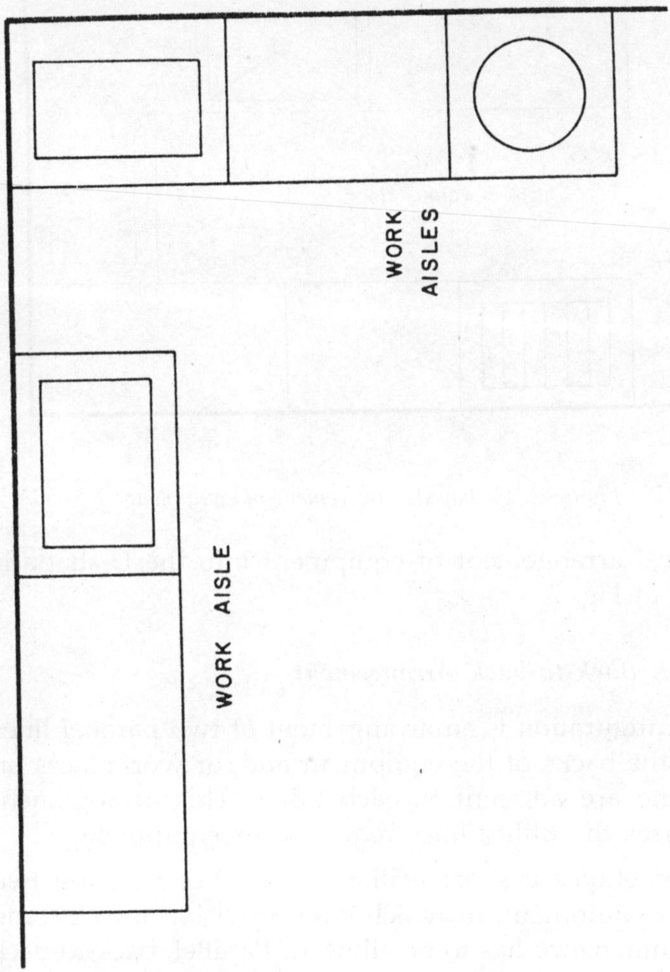

Figure 1. L-shaped arrangement of equipment.

only one or two employees are working. One disadvantage of this configuration is that straight-line flow through the area is not possible

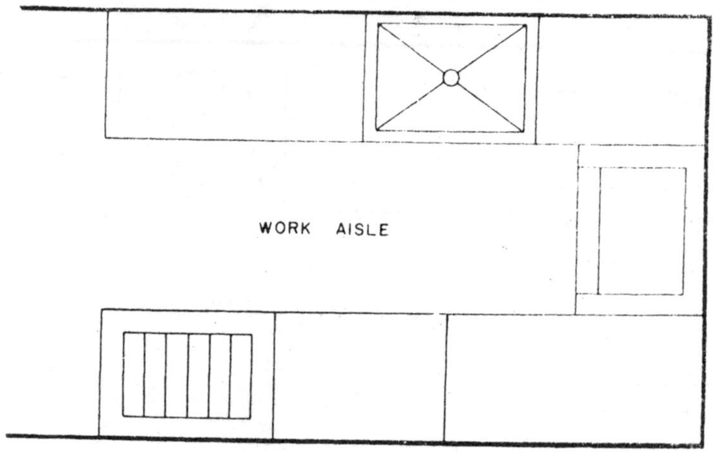

Figure 2. U-shaped arrangement of equipment

A typical arrangement of equipment into the U-shape is shown in Fig. 2.

Parallel, Back-to-back Arrangement

This configuration is an arrangement of two parallel lines where the backs of the equipment and/or workplaces on each line are adjacent to each other. This arrangement centralises the utility lines required for equipment.

Sometimes a short wall is placed between the two rows of equipment, in which case provision for cleaning and maintenance has to be allowed. Parallel, back-to-back arrangement of cooking equipment that must be vented is ideal because a single canopy hood can be used. The separation of major groups of equipment is easily accomplished with this configuration.

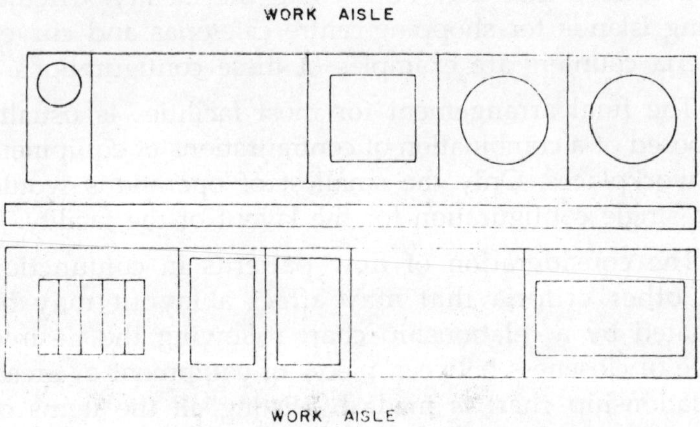

Figure 3. Parallel, back-to-back arrangement of equipment

Figure 3 illustrates parallel, back-to-back arrangement.

Parallel, Face-to-face Arrangement

This arrangement utilises two straight lines of equipment and workplaces where the fronts face each other and are separated by an aisle space. This is a very common configuration that can be used in many areas of the facility. A variation of this configuration is obtained by arranging a straight line of worktables between the two rows of equipment. The parallel, face-to-face arrangement requires two separate utility lines for equipment, as compared to the single utility line used in the parallel, back-to-back arrangement. Figure 4 shows the parallel, face-to-face arrangement.

Modifications of any of these configurations can be used to handle special cases and problems. Tee-shaped, open-square, or other configurations should be used if they result in the best solution to the layout problem. Curved or circular configurations are sometimes used, but they should be planned very carefully to fit straight-line configurations that may be used in the facility. Circular serving islands for shopping-centre cafeterias and curved cafeteria counters are examples of these configurations.

The final arrangement for most facilities is usually composed of a combination of configurations of equipment and workplaces. Only the smallest of operations would use a single configuration for the layout of the facility.

The consideration of flow patterns in conjunction with other criteria that may affect a layout may be evaluated by a relationship chart following the desired degree of closeness between pieces of equipment or areas. A relationship chart is made by listing all the items or areas to be arranged for a given facility. Closeness ratings for all pairs of trays are identified in the relationship chart. These ratings are based on number of factors including flow, efficient use of equipment, efficient use of utilities, use of labour, safety, and even the personal references of the planner. In the majority of the cases flow will still be the primary basis for the closeness ratings. Closeness ratings may be expressed by a numerical scale as shown text. The ratings are used to express the desired closeness for the final arrangement of the areas.

The usefulness of the relationship chart is dependent upon the planners' awareness of the need to compromise. Indicating that all areas of a facility have to be close to all other areas negates the purpose of the relationship chart. A suggested relationship chart of areas for one type of food service facility is shown in Fig. 5. It is important to note that other types of food service facilities may have a greater or fewer number of areas listed on the left side of the chart. In some cases areas may be combined as illustrated by this facility that will utilise one area for both salad and vegetable preparation.

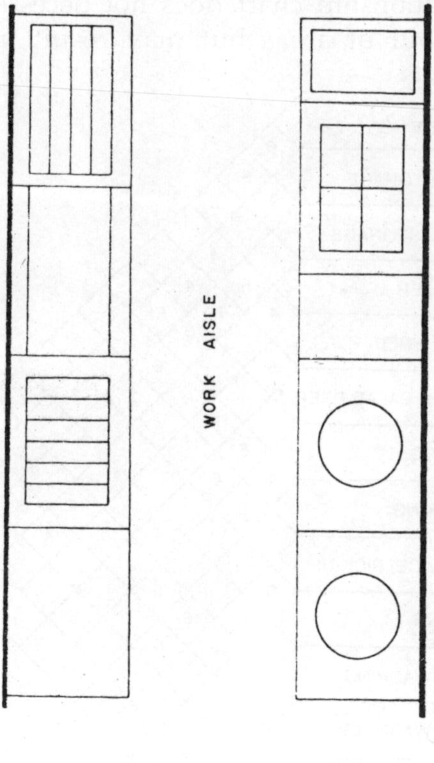

Figure 4. Parallel, face-to-face arrangement of equipment

In other instances, additional areas may be designated as occurs when a separate take-out area is to be planned for in addition to the regular service area. Thus each different project to be planned requires a different relationship chart depending on the defined areas to be considered. If the exact or approximate size and shape of each area including aisle spaces are known, a preliminary schematic can be developed from the relationship chart ratings. The relationship chart does not necessarily lead to just one layout of areas but may result in several alternative layouts.

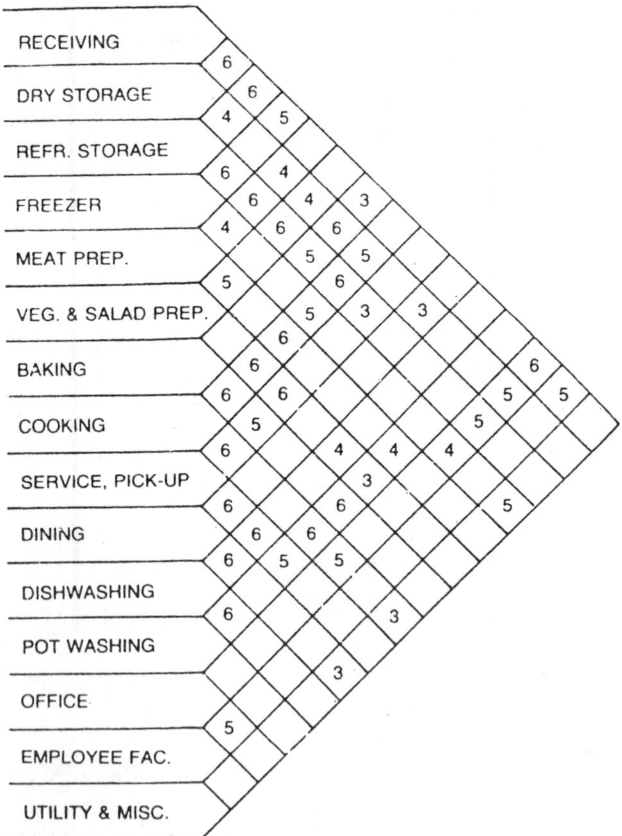

Figure 5. Relationship chart with closeness ratings for a typical food service facility

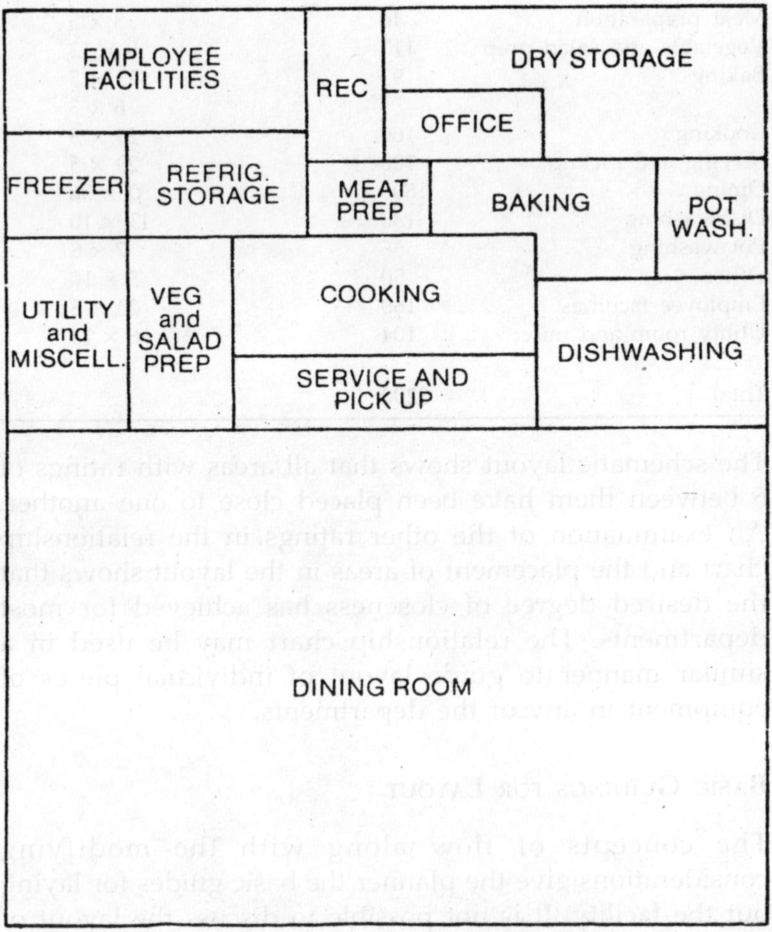

Figure 6. Schematic layout based on relationship chart closeness ratings

One schematic layout of the areas identified in the relationship chart is shown in Fig. 6. The areas and sizes of each department used to develop the layout are follows:

Department	Ft²	Dimensions
Receiving	50	5 × 10
Dry storage	200	20 × 10
Refrigerated storage	84	12 × 7
Freezer	56	8 × 7

Meat preparation	40	8 × 5
Vegetable and salad prep	117	9 × 13
Baking	93	15 × 5
		6 × 3
Cooking	160	20 × 8
Serving and pickup	100	20 × 5
Dining	1800	50 × 36
Dishwashing	130	13 × 10
Pot washing	56	7 × 8
Office	50	5 × 10
Employee facilities	160	20 × 8
Utility room and misc.	104	8 × 13
Total	3200	

The schematic layout shows that all areas with ratings of 6 between them have been placed close to one another. An examination of the other ratings in the relationship chart and the placement of areas in the layout shows that the desired degree of closeness has achieved for most departments. The relationship chart may be used in a similar manner to guide layout of individual pieces of equipment in any of the departments.

Basic Guidings for Layout

The concepts of flow along with the modifying considerations give the planner the basic guides for laying out the facility. It is not possible to discuss the layout of all areas for all types of food facilities, but general guides to the arrangement of some areas common to most facilities will be given. Overall design of the facility is usually based on the flow of major food items. Since most food items are received and then stored before preparation, the dry, refrigerated, and freezer storage areas should be adjacent to receiving areas and also be readily accessible to the various preparation areas.

The main cooking area is so located as to receive the flow from the preparation areas and have an outlet directly the serving area. The salad and sandwich preparation areas may so placed that their flow of foods is directly into the serving area. Placement of the dining area adjacent to the serving area is obvious. The flow of nonfood items is next evaluated to locate other areas. The flow of dinnerware in a repetitive route from serving areas to tying areas and then back to serving areas requires the dishwashing area to be adjacent to both. Similarly, the flow of utensils dictates Being the pot- and pan-washing section near the main cooking, baking, and serving areas.

Design of Storage Area

Layout of storage areas is based on convenience and accessibility. Arrangements that allow heavy and bulky materials to be moved title and as easily as possible are preferred. Central storage facilities with several satellite locations are good arrangements for many types of facilities. The storage space in the preparation, processing, and other functional areas should be planned so they do not interfere with efficient work methods. The use of combination walk-in and each-in storage units may increase the convenience of these areas. It is best to plan walk-in storage areas in a manner which keeps the products at least 8 in. (203 mm) above the floor to facilitate cleaning.

An alternative would be to use mobile bins and containers that can be easily moved when the area is cleaned. Storage areas for non-food supplies may be located in the various functional areas as required. Storage space for china, glass, and silverware may be provided in serving or dining areas. Linen and paper goods used for service are also stored in or near these areas.

Design of Cooking Area

Laying out the main cooking area is the key to fast and

efficient production of foods. The flow patterns affecting this area include inflow of foods from storage and preparation areas and utensils from the pot- and pan-washing area. Outflow of foods to the serving, salad preparation, and sandwich preparation areas is common. The cooking equipment should be arranged so that the most frequently used pieces are close to the pick-up location. Other factors related to the design of the main cooking area include the following:

— All heat- and moisture-producing equipment, such as fryers, broilers, griddles, ranges, and steamers, should be placed under ventilating hoods or be equipped with individual venting systems.

— Steam cooking equipment requires special installation including depressed floors, or the use of curbs.

— Some types of equipment require air for ventilation or cooling of enclosed spaces; vents and grill openings should not be blocked by other pieces of equipment.

— Provision has to be made to permit venting of fuel-burning equipment directly to the outside.

— Location of the main building ventilation or air-conditioning inlets is important to effect adequate cooling of the air without cooling the cooking equipment or interfering with the equipment venting system.

— If remote banquet rooms are to be served, methods of transporting hot foods and appropriate space for loading have to be considered.

— The use of partially or fully preprocessed foods will increase the need for refrigerated space in the cooking areas.

Flexibility and efficient use of employees and equipment can be obtained in some operations where similar equipment is involved in baking and cooking. In this case the baking and cooking areas are placed in close proximity so that kettles, ovens, and mixers can serve both areas. This may even result in reduced exhaust requirements. Placing the baking and cooking areas adjacent to each other also guides the placement of the pot-washing area since these two areas generate the bulk of the soiled pots.

The layout of preparation areas is fairly easy because most of the functions performed in them follow a logical sequence, and thus the equipment is arranged in the same sequence. Vegetable preparation, for example, basically involves trimming, washing, and size reduction, in that order. A straight-line arrangement of a work table for trimming, a sink for washing and draining, and equipment for size reduction becomes the layout for the area.

Since the inflow of vegetables is from storage areas, the trimming table is placed close to them; consequently, the size-reduction equipment is placed near the main cooking and salad preparation areas. Provision for temporary storage of materials and removal of waste will complete the layout of the vegetable preparation area for a small facility.

Salad preparation areas are planned in a similar manner. The foods should flow in a continuous path from the start of the preparation tasks, through the various workplaces and equipment, which are arranged in the order of the steps required, and on to the serving area. Operations that prepare a large number of the same or very similar salads may be designed by the concepts of mass assembly.

Design of Baking Areas

The volume and variety of baked items that will be produced in a particular food service operation determines the layout to be used. Operations that produce a minimum number of items such as pastries and desserts can combine the baking area with the cooking area. Employees' work shifts may be scheduled to avoid problems of equipment usage. Operations that will be involved in the production of a moderate amount of baked goods frequently locate the baking area adjacent to the cooking area so some equipment can be shared. Food service operations that will produce the full line of baked items including breads, rolls, pastries, or even speciality items may need a separate baking area in order to minimise interference between the cooking and baking functions.

The design of baking area layouts should follow the typical processing steps to assure a smooth work flow. For example, a proof box located near the ovens simplifies the loading of items into the ovens. Similarly, a landing table placed near the ovens simplifies unloading. Baker's tables are centrally located with easy access to storage areas, mixers, and kettles, as well as the proof box and ovens. Sufficient space is provided for mixing, cutting, panning, rolling, and finishing the baked items. Storage space for baking supplies, utensils, and tools that are frequently used are best located at the work centers.

Provision for storage of the finished baked items might take the form of mobile units for easy movement to the serving or pick-up areas. Another possibility would be to use pass-through storage units between the baking and serving areas. Special requirements such as the freezing and storage of some baked items are considered so that space for freezers is provided either in or near the baking areas. Refrigerators are required for the storage of highly perishable items such as custard-filled or whipped cream desserts.

Design of Serving Space

The layout of serving areas is based on the method and speed of service desired. Serving equipment should be arranged in the order of use, and should be located so they are easily accessible to serving personnel.

Table Service

Hot food pick-up areas are located adjacent to the main cooking battery. Provisions for maintaining the temperature of hot foods at pick-up areas should be considered. Additional serving stations or pantries for salads, desserts, rolls, and beverages are located nearer the dining area to avoid congestion. Linen, flatware, water, and butter used for setups are best placed in inconspicuous areas of the dining room. These stations may also include facilities for depositing soiled linen and tableware.

Counter Service

Most of the cooking and serving facilities in typical counter-service operations occur at the back bar opposite the dining counter. A common layout is to have a straight-line back bar with straight-line or a series of U-shaped dining counters. Some operations offering a more extensive menu may require additional preparation and cooking facilities that can be located in a separate area. An efficient layout in this case is to have the pick-up counter as a part of the back bar. This is also a good arrangement for operations having both counter and table-service sections. The pick-up area should be located for easy access to the table servers.

Cafeteria Service

Cafeteria counters are placed as close to the production areas as possible with due regard to the free flow of customers or users. The layout of cafeteria counters is based on the shape of the serving area and the anticipated traffic patterns. Counters may be arranged in a straight line, L-shaped, U-shaped, hollow square, or combinations of these configurations, as dictated by the length of counter required. The design of the counter should allow displayed foods that are usually selected in combination to be placed together on the counter.

Merchandising concepts call for desserts and salads to be located at the beginning of the line; hot foods should be at the end of the line to minimise cooling. Special care is needed in providing for cashiering, since this is one of the bottleneck areas in commercial cafeterias. The entire design of the cafeteria service system is based on volume flow, and anything that will speed service should be incorporated into the layout. Silver, napkins, water, and condiments may be located in stations away from the main counter area.

Islands placed between the serving and dining areas are frequently used for this purpose. Self-dispensing equipment for beverages will also help speed the flow of people. Cook-to-order items cause delays and are best located in a separate area where patrons can pull out of the main stream of flow to wait for their orders. This can be easily accomplished with the open square arrangement of counters.

The layout of dishwashing areas should follow the sequence of operations performed in washing. The arrangement has to provide for sorting, scraping or preflushing, and stacking, prior to loading the dishwashing machine. If glasses and silverware are to be washed separately, provisions for these operations have to be planned. Preflushing of soiled dishes may be accomplished in one of two ways. One method is to use a continuous flow of water over the dishes as they are being scraped. A disposal unit is used to handle the food wastes. The other method uses an overhead spray and is suitable for dishes that are placed in dish racks. In either case, the soiled-dish table has to be designed so that water is quickly drained away. Raised edges on the table help prevent excess water spillage.

Regardless of the type of dishwashing machine used, space for loading and unloading must be arranged. Rack-type machines are frequently loaded in a straight-line flow from the soiled-dish table. Rackless or peg-type machines require space for the loader to handle the individual pieces of dinnerware. Clean-dish areas are arranged so adequate drying time is allowed before the removal and stacking of dinnerware takes place.

The flow of dinnerware through the dishwashing area is planned to be continuous and over the shortest possible distance. The layout of other areas for the food facility should be accomplished in the same manner as given in the above examples. When all the preceding steps of the planning process are satisfactorily completed, the layout step becomes fairly easy.

8

Designing of Food Processing Facility

Design and construction of a food processing facility requires a great deal of planning. Information must be collected from many sources and combined into documents that are simple to read and share with others. Planning sessions should involve persons that represent all aspects of facility activity. Examples are production, maintenance, supervision, sales, accounting, receiving, warehousing, distribution, human resources, management, engineering, research and development, key suppliers (products and services), government agencies, and consultants.

Consultants include engineers, lawyers, insurance providers, and other specialists that may not be regularly employed by the company. For large projects, it is recommended to hold scheduled planning sessions at a convenient location that is free from distractions. It is often desirable to obtain an unrelated, third party to lead and moderate planning sessions inorder to retain objectivity and purpose. An agenda should be drafted for each planning session.

There are many of the elements to consider when designing food-processing plants. Since each situation is unique, some elements will not apply and some important elements may need to be added. Relevant elements can form the basis for a planning session agenda Elements listed are not in any particular order of importance and emphasise engineering design (not economics, marketing, logistics, and other necessary inputs). Lists of design considerations are given under four headings.

— Facility
— Process
— Product
— Other

Facility

1. Site selection: Identify the best location(s) for the facility, considering the following factors.
   — Economic development assistance -grants or other support offered to new businesses
   — Flexibility
   — Expansion
   — Utilities availability
   — Maintenance
   — Sanitation
   — Access
   — Environmental impact
   — Zoning laws
   — Permit requirements
   — Parking for employees and delivery vehicles
2. Existing or proposed facility size (square feet)
   — Designate size of dedicated areas (storage, cooler, processing, packaging, etc.)

— Provide a plan view of the proposed facilities layout (a scaled drawing is not necessary if dimensions are included)

— Estimate expansion requirements (show on drawing)

3. Provide a budget estimate for the cost of the facility
4. Utilities: Identify source(s) and cost to provide utility service. Review the impact of variable demand charges (if any) and limitations on quantity (e.g. BOD of discharge to treatment system). Consider including meters that can record utility usage to provide data for improving operating efficiency.
5. List code and permit requirements (local, state, federal, and international)
6. Type of construction (steel frame, concrete, panel, prepackaged, etc.)
7. Overhead clearance available or required in designated areas (especially processing)
8. Description of access requirements to facility and dimensions of openings
9. Flooring, walls, and ceiling in wash down and special use areas
10. Floor drains in wash-down and process areas
11. Type (drop-down, floor, or wall) and number of utilities connections (electric, steam, water, air, etc.) in process areas
12. Refrigerated storage requirement (square feet or amount of products/materials/pallets) for proper handling, rotation, and placement of goods

    — Temperatures

    — Raw materials (ingredients)

    — Finished product

— Rework

— Long term storage requirements for seasonal goods

— Stack height

13. Strategy for grouping separate refrigerated areas to maximise energy efficiency, materials handling requirements, and expansion needs
14. Ambient temperature storage requirement (square feet or amount of products/materials/pallets)

— Raw materials (ingredients)

— Finished product

— Packaging materials

— Rework

— Long-term storage for seasonal products (estimate)

— Incoming materials inspection and storage

— Wall clearance and inspection lane requirements

— Stack height to Develop a strategy for grouping separate storage areas to maximise materials handling requirements and expansion needs

15. Employee service facilities requirements

— Drinking water fountains

— Toilet and lavatory facilities

— Change rooms

— Training or class room

— Retiring room

— First aid

— Food service

16. All warehousing and storage areas

— Incoming materials inspection and storage

— Truck and railcar parking and sanitation facilities

— Wall clearance and inspection lane requirements
— Protective guard posts for walls, doors, and equipment

17. Cleaning and Sanitation
    — Layout
    — Materials handling
    — Grease trap location
    — Building exterior
    — Floors and drains
    — Walls and ceilings
    — Ventilation
    — Lighting
    — Pest proofing
    — Surface treatments and coatings
    — Truck and railcar sanitation
    — Wastewater pretreatment
    — Secondary and tertiary wastewater treatment systems
18. Process electrical equipment rating (wash-down, dust proof, explosion proof, etc.)
19. Electrical switch gear and motor control room location
20. Emergency Power: Indicate the amount (square feet orpercentage of area) and temperature of refrigerated ware-house or facility area to be protected by an emergencypower source, if any.
21. Parking and access
    — Delivery trucks
    — Truck drivers lounge
    — Railcar

— Employee

— Special designation (inspector, visitor, customer, etc.)

PROCESS

1. Describe value-added products to be processed.
2. Process organisation and flow
   - — Materials flow (product, waste, rework, packaging,ingredients, and intermediates) and storage
   - — Personnel flow
   - — Data collection and manipulation
3. Provide recipes and examples of product/packaging materials if available.
4. Regulatory requirements for products (local, state, federal, and international)
5. Describe the level of process automation desired for the facility (e.g. manual, semi-automated, or fully automated)
6. Describe the level of packaging automation desired for the facility (e.g. manual, semi-automated, or fully automated)
7. Describe the carton or case requirements for products
8. Describe the image desired for the facility (e.g. state-of-the-art, modern, or utility)
9. Provide a budget estimate for capital equipment expense
10. Is used equipment acceptable/desired? If so, state any specific areas in the process where used equipment is unacceptable

11. How will ingredients or raw materials be delivered to the facility (delivery size, pallet or container size, stacking specifications, temperature, frequency, supply capability, and plans for handling)?
12. How will packaging materials be delivered to the facility (delivery size, frequency, pallet dimensions, stacking specifications, case size, and plans for handling)?
13. How will finished goods leave the facility (frequency, pallet requirement, wrapping, coding, and handling requirement)?
14. Technology
    - Process equipment
    - Materials handling (pneumatic conveying, bucket elevators, augers, conveyors, gravity slide, etc.)
    - Control systems for process and environment (degree of automation)
    - Quality assurance (in house systems)
    - Research and development
15. Expansion capability and space availability.
16. Flexibility (change overs, seasonal packs or products, and future upgrades)
17. Reliability of equipment (lifetime requirement)
18. Waste treatment, handling, disposal, and recovery
19. Sanitation standards
    - Housekeeping
    - Raw materials handling and storage
    - Processed and finished product handling and storage
    - Waste handling procedures
    - Current Good Manufacturing Practices (cGMPs)

20. Sanitary facilities
    - Cleaning and Sanitising
    - Methods required
    - Systems needed
21. Personnel safety
22. Environmental safety
23. Product and process safety
    - Metal detection
    - Line magnets and strainers
    - cGMPs

PRODUCT

Describe the value-added products to be processed. Describe the physical properties of ingredients, intermediate and final product(s) (include or forecasting redients in future plans). Intermediate products may be important in cases where physical properties of the intermediates are unique when compared to the ingredients and final product. Examples of descriptive terms follow:

1. Common name of ingredient, source, or specification
2. Density (weight per volume)
3. Corrosive nature
4. Viscosity (indicate temperature or range of temperatures)
5. Sensitivity to air
6. Sensitivity to temperature
7. Sensitivity to moisture
8. Sensitivity to materials (contact)

9. Requirement for agitation or mixing
10. Dustiness
11. Flammability
12. Volatility
13. Reactivity
14. Bridging
15. Abrasive nature
16. Toxicity
17. Freezing point
18. Boiling point
19. Rheology
20. Particle size
21. Stiffness
22. Thermal conductivity
23. Electrical conductivity
24. Specific heat.

9

TEMPORARY FOOD SERVICE OPERATIONS

A temporary food service concession is a food establishment that operates at a fixed location for a period of time not more than 14 consecutive days in conjunction with a single event or celebration, such as a

— fair
— festival
— carnival
— circus
— regatta
— or similar transitory gathering

Each food concession in operation during an event open to the public must obtain a permit from the Local authorities.

For example in USA it is recommended that the application be returned to the Local Health Department (with fee if required) at least 3 weeks before the event. This allows time for the Sanitarian to adequately review the application and to advise you of necessary changes well in advance of the event. Applications may be obtained from any Local Health Department.

You must apply for a permit in order for the Local Health Department to review the proposed operation. The Sanitarian will work with you to review the following:

— Concession construction
— Types of foods to be prepared
— How the food will be prepared
— Methods to keep foods hot and cold
— Handwashing
— Utensil washing

The Sanitarian may also make suggestions that will enable your booth to operate more efficiently and safely.

Waste Management

— Provide adequate number of durable, lined garbage containers large enough for your needs
— Dispose of solid waste appropriately
— Discharge liquid waste into a sanitary sewer or collect in portable container and dispose of at approved location
— Do not dump liquid waste into streets, storm drains, creeks, or onto the ground
— Do not put discarded grease in the sanitary sewer—allow to harden and place in garbage

Concession Construction

— Locate concession away from sources of contamination such as animals, barns and petting zoos.

— Covered structure required to protect from windblown dust and debris, weather, insects, and animals
— Cleanable floors. Concrete or machine-laid asphalt is acceptable. No dirt, plastic, or canvas floors.
— Protect against insects by use of screens, fans, air curtains, or closable service openings
— Provide adequate lighting and properly shield bulbs

Potentially Hazardous Food

Potentially hazardous food is any food that requires temperature control because it is in a form capable of supporting the rapid and progressive growth of infectious or toxigenic microorganisms, such as eggs, meat, poultry, fish, and dairy foods. Examples are hamburgers, tacos, hot dogs, chili, and cream pies. Raw seed sprouts, cooked rice, potatoes, and beans are also considered to be potentially hazardous because they will support rapid bacterial growth.

Non-Potentially Hazardous Food

Non-potentially hazardous food includes fruit pies, dry goods and cereals, unconstituted dehydrated foods and baked goods. Other examples are cookies, breads, cakes, potato chips, popcorn, cotton candy, and candy bars.

Foodborne Illness

Foodborne illness is caused by consuming contaminated foods or beverages. Many different disease-causing microbes, or pathogens, as well as poisonous chemicals, can contaminate food. Common symptoms include diarrhea, abdominal cramping, fever, headache, vomiting, severe exhaustion, and sometimes blood or pus in the stools.

It come from raw animal foods, such as meat, poultry and eggs, are most likely to be contaminated. Fresh produce such as lettuce, tomatoes, sprouts, and melons may also present a food safety hazard. Even cooked, ready-to-eat foods can become cross-contaminated with bacteria transferred from raw products or from food handlers with poor personal hygiene. Proper cooking temperatures will destroy pathogens, and proper holding temperatures will control their multiplication.

Following points helps to reduce the risks:

1. Avoid cooling & reheating foods: Use canned products, like chili or refried beans, instead of preparing from scratch, cooling, and reheating.
2. Avoid hot holding of foods: Cook foods like tacos, burritos and shish kabob to order rather than cooking ahead of time and hot holding.
3. Minimise preparation: Use store-bought cole slaw, potato, macaroni, or pasta salads instead of preparing them yourself.
4. Do not touch ready-to-eat food with bare hands: Use utensils such as deli paper, spatulas, tongs, or single-use gloves.

Equipment

- Smooth, easily cleanable, and in good repair
- Kept clean and sanitised
- For customer self-service, single service articles should be individually wrapped or in an approved dispenser
- Do not re-use aluminum foil pans, tin cans, bread wrappers, single service items
- Store in-use serving utensils:
  - In the food with the handle above top of food and container

— On clean portion of table, equipment. (Clean and sanitise utensils every 4 hours.)

— In a running water dipper well for ice cream utensils

Dishwashing Facilities

— Use clean, warm water

— Use a three compartment sink or three clean containers:

— Wash

— Rinse

— Sanitise (½ tablespoon of liquid bleach added to one gallon of water)

— Air Dry (do not towel dry)

— Use appropriate test strips

— Rinse and store wiping cloths in a separate bucket of sanitiser

— Store detergents and sanitisers separately from food and single service articles

Facilities for Handwashing

— Warm water

— Soap

— Individual paper towels

— Bucket to collect dirty water

For example, an air pump thermos or jug of warm water with a turn spout may be used to dispense warm water.

Concession Workers

— Wear hair restraints, clean clothes: No jewelry except plain ring.

— Wash hands frequently:
  a) Before starting work
  b) After smoking, eating, or drinking
  c) After using the restroom
  d) Before putting on gloves
  e) After handling raw products
  f) When contaminated
— Do not smoke or eat while working
— Do not work if you are sick or have open sores or cuts on your hands or arms
— Do not touch ready-to-eat foods with bare hands
— Obtain foodhandler's card if required by the Local Health Dept.
— Designate a Person-In-Charge (PIC). A PIC must be present and must know food safety rules

Food Source

Home canned and home prepared foods, ice made at home, raw milk, or storage of prepared foods at private homes are not allowed.

Food Protection

— Cover, protect foods on display. Do not allow customers to help themselves to open, unprotected containers.
— Provide condiments, such as ketchup, mustard, coffee creamer, and sugar in dispensers, individual packets or squeeze or pump containers.
— Store foods at least 6 inches off the floor/ground.
— Protect foods from contamination and maintain at proper temperatures during transportation and storage.

— Do not store packaged food in water or undrained ice.
— Protect against insects by use of screens, fans, air curtains, or closable service openings.
— Use a scoop or an automatic dispenser to fill cups with ice.
— Do not use a cup as an ice scoop.

Food Temperatures

Potentially hazardous foods must be stored at temperatures below 41°F (under refrigeration) or above 140°F (hot holding) at all times, except when undergoing preparation or cooking. Do not store potentially hazardous food at room temperature. Food products found in the temperature danger zone are subject to embargo or destruction.

Thawing

Do not thaw foods at room temperature. Thaw foods as part of a cooking process; under refrigeration at 41°F or below; under cold running water (70°F or less); or in the microwave oven with immediate transfer to conventional cooking.

Thermometers

All refrigerators and cold holding units must have an accurate, visible thermometer. A product thermometer is also needed to check food temperatures. Clean and sanitise before each use. Thermometers may be purchased from restaurant supply companies or from large department stores. Non-digital thermometers should be marked off in 2° increments. For thin foods, like hamburger patties, insert thermometer sideways or use tip-sensitive device.

10

Mobile Food Service Units

"Mobile food service unit" means an approved movable vehicle or cart that is operated from either a fixed location or on an established daily route; is supplied from, and cleaned, maintained and stored at a commissary or base of operation; and from which food is prepared, served, or provided for the public with or without charge.

Mobile food service units are not movable restaurants. Because facilities are extremely limited, food preparation is restricted. Not all foods are suitable for mobile food service. The person in charge of a mobile food unit must operate the mobile food unit from an approved commissary or servicing area and shall return to such location for supplies, thorough cleaning, and other servicing activities, as approved in a plan of operation.

When not in use a mobile unit must be stored at an approved servicing area or other approved location. All requirements are based on the menu and preparation procedures on the mobile food service unit. A definite menu must be set. Design requirements of the mobile unit vary with the type of food (hazardous or nonhazardous) and whether the food is pre-packaged or not. All mobile food service units are evaluated on an individual basis. All new operations require complete mobile plan review regardless of whether the unit has had a permit before or not. In U.S.A., the plan review fee is $432.00 for a new operation. Information necessary for plan review includes:

— ownership information,
— menu,
— design of the mobile food service unit,
— commissary, and/or base of operation,
— site location/itinerary and
— operating procedures.

Plan Review Requirements

A. *Ownership Information*: List name of the mobile food service unit and location for the unit, the owner's name, home address and phone number.

B. *Menu*: List all food and beverages to be served. Include whether foods are packaged or how foods are dispensed. Prepackaged foods are preferred and may be required. Some foods are exempt from code, such as commercially prepared and prepackaged non-potentially hazardous foods. Outline food preparation procedures according to your menu. Note all steps in the preparation of each menu item, including condiments, at the commissary and on the vehicle when applicable. Detail how food is prepared, when it is made, how it is packaged, etc. All food items used or sold must be from an approved source. Use of food prepared in unapproved kitchens or living quarters is not allowed.

C. *Design of Cart/Vehicle*: Basic design is up to the owner. A picture of the mobile cart is required. A scale drawing, including all views is required (top view, front view, side view, elevation). Overhead protection is required. Specify all equipment on cart/vehicle, such as temperature control equipment, plumbing fixtures, tanks, water heater, etc. Include spec sheets for equipment. Note surface finish on plan—all surfaces must be smooth, sealed and easy to clean.

D. *Commissary*: The commissary, or base of operations, is an essential part of a mobile unit's operation. Even if the commissary is already a licensed facility, plans for the commissary must accompany the mobile plan for review. All facilities and operations must meet requirements of the Food Code. A copy of the commissary plan must be included in the mobile plans. The commissary must provide adequate storage for all supplies, including refrigeration if required. Minimum plumbing requirements for a commissary include a 3-compartment sink or other approved dishwashing facilities, a mopsink and, if food preparation occurs at the commissary, a hand sink. Cleaning and sanitising required on a daily basis for all equipment, utensils, water tanks and the cart.

   The commissary must be at one location, not the sinks in one place and storage at another. The commissary must also include space for cleaning and overnight storage of the cart. Note on your plans how commissary access is achieved—i.e., size of doorways, halls, radius of corners, etc. Be prepared to show mobility of the cart to the commissary upon request. The operator must have access to the commissary during all hours of operation. If commissary is another food service, explain how both businesses will use the facilities. Commissary keys must be provided if business hours of the cart are longer than the commissary's.

E. *Site Location/Itinerary*: Mobile carts must have an exact location for their operation. A site map must show the cart location in relationship to streets, buildings, etc. Also, show the distance from the site location to the commissary. Provide a letter of restroom availability giving permission for employees to use a public restroom within 200 feet during the business hours of the cart. The distance is the usual route a person would take to reach the restroom. Site locations on public property may require a street use permit. Contact the city or county agency where you plan on locating. Mobile vehicles operation at a specific location follow the same requirements as above for carts.

Mobile vehicles who have a daily route must submit an itinerary of their locations specifying exact locations and times, hours of operation, and when the vehicle/ employee will be back at the commissary. Mobile vehicles must provide letters of restroom availability for each stop that lasts longer than 1 hour.

F. *Operating Procedures*: Note business hours and time at the commissary. Submit an outline of your daily activities. Start with preloading of the unit, transport to site location, set-up on site, your operation during business hours, continuous cleaning and sanitising procedures while operating, etc. For the end of the business day, outline closing procedures for unit, transport back to commissary, unloading of cart, storage of supplies (i.e., food, paper products, utensils), cleaning and sanitising procedures, maintenance of water and waste water tanks, and cart storage.

Specific Requirements

Mobile Food Carts

Carts are limited to serving only hot dogs, espresso, beverages and non-potentially hazardous foods with limited food preparation; i.e., fresh squeezed high acid juices, or snow cones. No preparation of potentially hazardous food is allowed on a mobile cart. A special exemption exists for hot dogs and for espresso carts for the preparation of milk.

Preparation and maintenance of food

a. All preparation, packaging of non-potentially hazardous foods and clean up must be done at the commissary or another commercial establishment. Proper food preparation procedures and adequate facilities must be used.

b. Hot dogs must be cooked to and hot held at 140 F or above. All warmed hot dogs left over at the end of the day must be discarded.

c. Milk for espresso must be steamed for immediate service only, then the pitcher placed in the refrigerator until the next order. Leftover steamed milk at the end of the day must be discarded.

d. Granita machines must maintain temperatures of 41°F or less. The machines must be cleaned and sanitised daily.

e. Juice preparation is limited to high acid juices, such as lemonade. Extractors are not allowed on carts because of the difficulty of cleaning them during operation. Blenders may be allowed with a variance.

f. Mechanical refrigeration is required for the milk and hot dogs. Temperatures must be kept at 41°F or less. Thermometers must be visible in all refrigeration units.

g. A metal stem type thermometer shall be accurate to ± 2°F and available to check food temperatures.

h. Only one extra ice chest will be allowed for non-hazardous beverages or other non-hazardous foods. Paper products may also be stored on this cart. All other food products and supplies must be stored on the main cart or in the commissary.

i. Microwave ovens are allowed for reheating of non-potentially hazardous foods for immediate service only.

j. Sanitised wiping cloths are required. Clean wiping cloths and sanitising solution must be on site. Soiled wiping cloths must be stored in a separate plastic bag. All work surfaces must be sanitised throughout the day.

k. Reusable utensils (i.e., tongs, spoons, etc.) must be washed and sanitised at the commissary. If the commissary is not convenient to carry out constant dish washing, then extra clean and sanitised utensils must be loaded on the cart in a sanitary plastic bag and soiled utensils must be replaced. Store dirty utensils in a separate plastic bag for washing and sanitising at the commissary.

l. No utensils are needed for prepackaged foods. The operator cannot package or handle unwrapped food. Only the customer can open the package.

m. Customer utensils must be single service and stored and dispensed in a sanitary manner.

n. Condiments must be prepackaged single servings or in dispenser bottles.

Sinks and water requirements

Sinks and water supply requirements for carts preparing or serving unwrapped foods include the following:

a. A handsink is required, with hot and cold or tempered running water (minimum 100° F), under pressure, with handsoap and paper towels. The handsink must be operational and easily accessible at all times while the cart is in operation. If handsinks are in cabinets or drawers, they must be left open to keep the handsink available. A minimum of 5 gallons of water is required for handwashing. Any additional water for use on the cart must be provided in addition to the water for handwashing.

b. Water supply for the handsink must be from an approved source (i.e., approved public water supply at commissary).

c. The waste water tank must be 15% larger than the fresh water supply tank.

d. The waste water tank must be emptied or drained at the commissary, or approved disposal site, never on the street or ground or used to water plants. If waste tanks are not removable, a drainage pad, graded and sewered, is required, as well as facilities for in-place cleaning and sanitising.

e. Tanks for water supply must be safe, durable, corrosion resistant, non-absorbent. Tanks for water supply and waste water shall be rigid, durable and cleanable. Collapsible tanks are not acceptable. Tanks must be easily cleanable.

f. A 3-compartment sink is not required on the cart, but must be available at the commissary.

Vehicles Serving Prepackaged Food

A vehicle or person serving prepackaged food and beverages pursuant to prearranged itineraries (specific routes) or at a fixed location. Peddling in residential areas is prohibited.

1. All preparation and packaging must be done at the commissary or another commercial establishment. Proper food preparation procedures and adequate

facilities must be used. Potentially hazardous foods must be at 41°F or less or 140°F or above while on the truck. Pre-chilling the refrigeration units prior to loading is required.

2. Mechanical refrigeration is preferred and may be required depending on menu (i.e., hazardous foods and length of business day). Refreezable or dry ice may be utilised in an ice chest, the inside and outside must be smooth, cleanable and durable. (Styrofoam ice chests are not approved).
3. Facilities for hot holding must maintain 140° F or above. Mechanical units are required, powered by propane, electricity or generators, etc. Thermostatic controls are recommended to adequately control hot holding temperature in variable weather conditions. Preheating the hot units prior to loading is required.
4. Reheating for hot holding is only allowed for foods that have been processed in a facility under WSDA, FDA, or USDA inspection. Facilities for reheating must rapidly reheat within one hour. Hot holding of reheated foods is not recommended. Reheating "to order" is a safer method and may be required. Potentially hazardous foods prepared in the commissary may be reheated for immediate service only.
5. Thermometers must be available in all cold holding units. A metal stem type thermometer must be available to check food temperatures for hot and cold foods.
6. No utensils are needed for prepackaged foods. The operator cannot open packages or handle unwrapped food. Only the customer can open the package.
7. Customer utensils must be single service and stored and dispensed in a sanitary manner.

8. Condiments must be prepackaged single servings or in dispenser bottles. Additional requirements for vehicles that stop at office buildings and sell prepackaged foods floor to floor:
   a. Mechanical refrigeration is preferred and may be required in vehicle. Refreezable ice packs may be utilised for floor to floor sales (no regular ice). Hot holding is not permitted.
   b. Condiments must be prepackaged single servings.
9. Prepackaged food must be properly labelled.

Vehicles Preparing or Serving Unpackaged Food

A vehicle preparing or serving food in an approved enclosed mobile unit which operates at a specified location or on a prearranged route. May serve non-potentially hazardous foods or may do limited preparation of potentially hazardous foods. Limited preparation means food preparation is simplified to reduce excessive steps where food may become contaminated (i.e., quick "cook and serve" or "assemble and serve" on order).

1. All preparation and packaging must be done in the commissary or another commercial establishment; i.e., chopping lettuce, cutting tomatoes, slicing meat, making soup. Minimal food preparation is allowed on the vehicle, but there may be additional requirements.
2. Mechanical refrigeration is required for all potentially hazardous foods. Cold potentially hazardous foods must be held less than 41°F. Prechilling the refrigeration units prior to loading is required.
3. Facilities for hot holding must maintain 140°F or above. Mechanical units are required, powered by propane, electricity, or generators. Preheating the hot units prior to loading is required

4. Cooking of raw meats on the vehicle is restricted to thin foods, such as, hamburger patties. Cooking of raw meats greater than one inch thick in thickness is not allowed.
5. Reheating for hot holding is only allowed for foods that have been processed in a facility under WSDA, FDA, or USDA inspection or foods that were cooked and cooled in an approved nonmobile food establishment. Facilities for reheating must rapidly reheat within one hour. Hot holding of reheated foods is not recommended. Reheating to order: is a safer method and may be required.
6. Cooling is not allowed for potentially hazardous foods on the vehicle. Leftover hot foods must be discarded.
7. All foods on the vehicle must be protected from contamination such as with sneeze guards, or dome shields.
8. Condiments must be in single service packages or dispenser bottles. Condiments unavailable in single service packaging and which can't be dispensed in bottles may be served in bulk, provided that the condiment is non-potentially hazardous and there is a sneeze guard for food protection (i.e., sauerkraut).
9. Customer utensils must be single service and stored and dispensed in a sanitary manner.
10. Thermometers must be available in all cold holding units. A metal stem type thermometer is required to check all food temperatures (hot and cold).
11. Sanitised wiping cloths are required. Clean wiping cloths and a sanitising solution must be on the vehicle. Soiled wiping cloths must be stored in a separate plastic bag.
12. All equipment and supplies must be stored on the mobile vehicle or in the commissary.

13. A handsink is required.
14. A 3-compartment dishwashing sink is required with potable hot and cold or tempered running water under pressure when utensils are reused on the mobile food unit.
15. Servicing areas are required for vehicles. If water tanks are refilled by hoses, the hoses must be food grade, retractable to facilitate sanitary storage off the ground, and used for no other purpose than for freshwater draw. All hoses must have vacuum breakers to prevent back siphonage. Hose connections to tanks must be tight and must quickly connect/release.
16. If RV dump sites are used for wastewater holding tank disposal, a letter of permission and site address for the facility must be provided. A mop sink must still be provided at the commissary for vehicle clean up.
17. Ventilation hoods are required for any grease producing cooking equipment. If deep fryers are utilised, a tight fitting, heat resistant cover shall be locked in place for safe transport of hot grease.

11

Food Service Operations in Schools

The food service industry as a whole is slow to change even when there are influences all around working to facilitate a change. It usually takes an act of government to bring about change in school food service programmes. From an educational viewpoint, school enrolment are fluctuating. School administrators are building new schools, closing old schools, and renovating other schools to meet the needs of student populations. Changes in school food service programmes resulting from current trends have taken on many forms.

Trends impacting the school food service programmes can be categorised as follows:

1. Customer expectations.
2. Alternate food production systems.
3. New technology.
4. Food safety initiative.
5. Manufacturing of food service equipment.
6. Equipment distribution.
7. Changes in regulations governing the food service programmes.

8. Changes in the leadership role of school food service programme professionals.

Customer Expectations

The customers have changed and will continue to change as they are influenced by the information age. Consider, too, the impact of choice on the customer - entertainment choice, dress choice, commercial food service choice. Students have higher expectations resulting from their dining-out experiences. Their expectations demand a wider variety of foods, better quality, increased food service choices, and an enhanced dining atmosphere. Menu demands include healthier foods, more "ethnic" menu items, and retail appeal.

Customer expectations drive changes in menu offerings, menu merchandising, programme marketing, production techniques, form of purchased food, and serving systems. Student customers whose expectations are not met will look to the competition for their food choices. Every school food service programme wants to keep customers. The competition with commercial enterprise has motivated directors to respond to the trends in displaying and serving foods. Speed of service, however, will always remain a key factor regardless of the type of service. Innovations in serving systems will impact equipment purchase decisions. Serving systems such as:

— Food court concepts students select from various specialty stations (as observed in local shopping malls) such as burger and fry bar, salad bar, pizza bar.

— Retail, commercial, and/or self-branding foods popular branding of fast food items or self-branding which usually includes school name or mascot.

— Kiosks a small, free-standing structure with one or more open sides used for point-of-service and point-of-sale.

— Packaged "componentised" meals prepackaged, reimbursable meals, pick-up and go, i.e., sandwich and fruit.
— Food boutiques a retail activity zone where specialised foods and meal components are served.
— Marché concepts based on European open-air marketplaces, the emphasis is on visual display, exhibition preparation, and random points of service.

The long term trend in school food service programmes will be a blend of self service and operator service with greater showcasing of food. This will include visible line-of-site preparation areas allowing for some part of the food preparation to be seen and appreciated by the student customer. Rounding out Trend 1 is the desire for food service operations to expand the use of school kitchens to prepare meals for non-student populations. If your programme provides meals to groups outside of the school population or is considering it in the next five years, you have an additional set of customer expectations to address in your purchase of food service equipment.

Remember the guiding principles. The challenge is to make equipment purchasing decisions with flexibility to meet future needs of your customers. This will allow operations to handle incoming fads and long-term trends while maintaining operation viability.

Alternate Food Production Systems

Programmes considering centralised food production systems must consider these factors in the decision-making and value-analysis process:

— make vs. buy.
— labour availability and cost (including benefits).
— menu flexibility requirements.

— cost control demands.

— space demands.

— quality control and "fresh prepared" expectations.

Once a decision is made to use a centralised food production facility, the next step is to select a food transportation system. Factors to consider in analysing a transport system for hot or cold foods include:

— satellite rethermalisation capabilities: Is there equipment located at the school site to reheat food that is transported cold?

— geographic boundaries, transportation times: Are the satellite school locations geographically close enough to transport food in a reasonable length of time while maintaining food in the appropriate hot or cold temperature zones?

— temperature retention and food safety considerations: Is transport equipment available to maintain appropriate hot or cold temperatures during the length of transportation to satellite schools?

— labour availability: Are qualified personnel available to transport food, receive food, finish preparation, and serve food items?

— cost: What is the initial start-up expense of a food transport system?

Programmes selecting a chilled food system have a variety of methods to consider:

— *Blast chill:* Foods are rapidly chilled by circulating cold air bringing the temperature from the appropriate internal temperature to 34°F within 90 to 120 minutes (commonly solid foods larger than 2 inches in diameter). This method is also used when smaller production needs are required on a variety of menu items.

— *Water bath chill:* Foods are rapidly chilled by circulating cold water in a contained tank bringing the temperature from appropriate degree of doneness to 34°F within 90 to 120 minutes. Items chilled are placed in plastic bags and securely closed. Liquid or partial liquid food items such as soups, stews, gravies, and sauces are chilled in tumble chillers. Meat roasts and whole poultry items may be chilled in bags in circulating cold water tanks.

— *Combination system* (blast and water bath): Both types of chilling equipment are available to chill the appropriate menu item.

— *Partial system*: This method addresses automated packaging with hot transport or blast chilled with chilled transport.

Rethermalisation methods will be implemented using conventional equipment such as combination ovens, convection ovens, steamers, kettles, and braising pans. Rethermalisation can also be accomplished using specialised equipment such as controlled humidity cabinets. In the coming years, you can expect variations of all types of systems to be implemented. There are no pure methods, and the needs of individual school systems vary.

Impacts of New Technologies

There are any number of new technologies that will impact current and future pieces of food service equipment.

— *Combination oven-steamer*: this equipment has been available but is just now gaining acceptance. Available in either gas or electric, these "work horses" provide speed, higher yields, food quality, less handling, ability to cook more than one food at a time with no flavour transfer, and ease of cleaning.

— *Induction cooking:* means instant heat with no open flames or hot spots (heats the food, not the kitchen) and it is easy to clean. Induction uses a magnetic field to "heat" the pan or pot while the unit itself stays cool. Look for induction cook tops, woks, griddles, and fryers.

— *Holding cabinets:* may seem to be the lowest tech equipment in the kitchen, but there is news in humidity control. By properly holding and controlling food, the texture of the food is maintained. Not all cabinets are the same and you should test before you buy.

— *Boiler-less and variable-temperature steaming:* provides speed and preserves colour, texture, and nutrients. There are a few new steamers that create saturated steam without a boiler. This cuts water, energy, and maintenance costs dramatically.

— *Hot air tumble fryer:* will produce very successful fries using a normal blanched fry with only 5% fat. An added benefit is that these fries can be reheated to fresh quality. Prices have fallen, but this item is still at a premium. However, if you also consider the oil, hood, and exhaust system savings, the payback can be relatively short.

— *Cooking with light:* has the speed of a microwave, yet cooks and browns naturally. For now, this type of oven can be used to prepare special meals or meals at odd hours.

— *Combination convection-microwave oven:* bakes a whole chicken in 18 minutes. You will find it has the speed of a microwave and the browning of a convection oven.

Food Safety Initiative

The practice of providing safe food makes good sense. With this in mind, the implementation of a Hazard Analysis Critical Control Point (HACCP) food safety system will eventually become enforced. It moves food safety from inspection to prevention. HACCP standards will influence all areas of the school food service operation such as:

— increased chilling requirements

— implementation of chilled food systems

— monitoring technology - method of tracking and documenting temperatures and times of food products whether in a cooking, chilling, reheating, transporting, or holding status

— greater emphasis being placed on the ease of cleaning and sanitising of all equipment and supplies

Look for the food safety initiative to impact equipment purchase decisions. Expect an increase in computer temperature tracking. This computer technology will provide a vital data link to monitor temperatures from the delivery of food products through receiving, production, and service. These data are an integral part of due diligence that is required to certify safe food.

Manufacturing of Food Service Equipment

Manufacturers face a substantial challenge. They want to produce quality equipment with value-added features while maintaining profitability. In turn they are expected to offer the equipment at an affordable price, even though the cost of manufacturing is very expensive. Few manufacturers use robotics. As a matter of fact, most food service equipment is made by hand including hand welding and hand polishing. Manufacturers address this challenge by implementing cost reductions and developing advancements.

In many cases, the cost reductions become an enhancement. Manufacturers strive to provide equipment that will withstand constant use by a variety of employees. Also, they strive to provide the most reliable component parts not only for the benefit of their customers but also to reduce warranty costs. For example, the trend to move to electro-processor based controls from electro-mechanical controls will become the standard.

Electro-processor based controls may be seen as digital read outs, touch pads, and computer programming options. These controls have become more reliable and multi-functional, and they require a smaller housing. The enhancement results in a smaller piece of equipment with the same or greater production capacity. The trend toward manufacturing equipment with built-in maintenance operations will be observed across the board in many types of equipment.

As it becomes a value-added feature, it will also reduce warranty cost. Manufacturers have learned that not everything has to be made of metal and stainless steel to exist successfully in a kitchen environment. New materials are being developed and used that are recognised as safe and more reliable. This cost reduction also becomes an enhancement. Manufacturers continue to meet the growing demands on environmental concerns. These concerns include energy usage, air quality, water quality, and water use.

Other concerns involve the work environment. Examples may include better safety features for the protection of the operator and better insulation to enhance the working climate. Manufacturers are responding to the needs of a diverse workforce and are offering universal or multilingual labels. Other trends in technology will emphasise interactive information - integrating point of sale (POS), production, and food safety monitoring functions. Manufacturers are introducing new types of production and service system equipment that will:

— meet customer expectations for food quality.

— incorporate flexibility for changing needs.

— require fewer employees to operate.

Manufacturers are not bound by "the way we have always done things." As a matter of fact, you may find a manufacturer that is willing to custom-design a piece of equipment to meet your innovation. Equipment design engineers are continuously developing and testing new food service systems to meet the needs of the everchanging food service environment.

The manufacturer's representative is a key player in identifying solutions to your equipment purchasing needs. Other sources of information include online resources, food service equipment shows, and professional journals. Food service equipment testing facilities also give you an opportunity to "test drive" the equipment before making a final purchasing decision.

Distribution of Equipment

Once food service equipment has been identified for specification, a source of distribution must be found. The channels of equipment distribution are changing. Traditionally, all food service equipment was purchased through a food service equipment dealer. Now other channels are available. For example, food service equipment can be purchased through a food distributor (broadline distributor) or directly from the manufacturer. If one of these channels is used, the dealer will be bypassed. The channel of distribution chosen by the school district will depend upon the specific needs of the purchaser, the accessibility of each option, and the experience of the buyer.

Influence of Regulations

The influence of regulations can affect equipment purchase decisions. For example, the United States Department of Agriculture has integrated the 1995 Dietary Guidelines for Americans into the Child Nutrition Programmes (CNP). The 'School Meals Initiative for Healthy Children' requires the school lunch programme over a week to:

— limit total fat to 30 percent of total calories.

— limit saturated fat to less than 10 percent of total calories.

— reduce the levels of sodium and cholesterol.

— increase the levels of dietary fibre.

Careful selection of food service equipment can be expected to enable compliance of the regulations by incorporating preparation methods to reduce fat. Regulations may also impact the food service equipment purchasing decision in the following ways:

— Production methods are determined by the dietary guidelines.

— Regulations on food safety and sanitation standards determine the required rate of rising or falling temperatures, hot-holding, and cold-holding capabilities.

— Regulations on environmental standards determine ventilation requirements, energy efficiency, and disposal of waste.

— Regulations on building codes and local health department codes may also impact the choice of food service equipment.

Regulations need to be considered early in the equipment purchasing process because they can limit the choices available to you. Each food service programme director must take responsibility to meet regulations and codes.

Changing Role of Food Service Professionals

The school food service programme director plays a crucial role in guiding the food service equipment purchasing process. It is up to the director to lead in the decision-making process. Keep in mind:

— You and your employees have the greatest insight into what types of equipment have and have not worked in the past.

— You have survey tools to determine customer expectations of the food service programme.

— You have an understanding of the regulations governing the school food service programme that no one else from the school system or outside the school system has.

— You bring to the planning team a level of expertise that no one else from the outside brings.

— You must convince the other interested parties that your guiding principles reflect what is truly best for your programme.

These trends should demonstrate the challenge that each director has to operate the food service system as a business within the educational arena. Your job is to visualise the impact of each trend on your food service programme in the next five years. The equipment purchasing decisions made today will impact outcomes from this point forward.

12

Food Service Facilities in Hospitals

Hospitals now face competition from a growing number of alternative health care facilities. These competitors include nursing homes, adult day care centers, retirement centers with acute care facilities, freestanding outpatient clinics, and independent home care agencies. There is continuing concern about the millions of people who do not have any form of health insurance or access to health care, as well as for the millions of others who have severely restricted or inadequate protection.

The health care field faces still other concerns. These include the growing number of persons affected with the human immunodeficiency virus (HIV), the increased number of people with tuberculosis (TB), the increased prevalence of child and spousal and drug abuse, the aging of the population, few medically trained personnel in geriatric medicine, and the emotional stress of daily living and working that takes its toll on health care providers. These external factors affect the internal operation of health care organisations. Many of these organisations are faced with shorter lengths of stay, reduced census, fewer payers, shortage of qualified personnel, increased paperwork and verification of services, and competition for customers.

They are also faced with meeting the increasing cost of providing quality service while still meeting the needs, wants, and perceptions of the customers.

As a result, many health care organisations are engaged in cost-effective programs that downsize the number of personnel, implement cross-functional training for the realignment of job duties, and combine elementary functions that may not meet the mission of the organisation (therefore reducing expense cost). This includes more outpatient procedures, less invasive procedures, and the increased use of technology. The aging of the population and the increased number of sophisticated older adults in residential health care services are additional causes for concern.

Changing Trends in Health Care Professionals

Changes are occurring almost minute by minute all across the world. Changes must happen for society to progress. Not all changes are due to the discoveries of scientists and advanced technology; some are due to the economic climate of the time and the desire for social equality. Change is the result of substitutions, disruptions, competition, or new developments; it is a difference in the way that things are done. One change in health care organisations may be seen in the way that care has shifted from a hospital base to outpatient departments, home health care providers, and other outreach centers. As these changes in organisation take place, specialists who deliver care in hospitals are refocusing the way they deliver this care. Many physicians are being trained to perform crossfunctional job duties.

Cross-functional training is the integration and progressive sequence of learning experience whereby employees are provided with the knowledge and skills needed to perform more than one function. Socioeconomic changes are taking place on a worldwide basis. The Berlin Wall fell fifteen years ago. The eastern communist nations are still seeking not only independence but improved financial and technical assistance from the more prosperous nations. The war in Iraq has cost many billions of dollars and the deaths of many U.S. soldiers and civilians. Problems still exist in Bosnia and Afghanistan, and changes are occurring now in the former Eastern Bloc such as the Russian-Chechnyan war. Wars and rumors of wars that use technological advances in weaponry are ever present.

Daily across the world, thousands of people die of malnutrition, natural disasters, and emerging pathogens. Transportation and communications are almost instantaneous. When an event happens on the opposite side of the world, we are able to see and hear about it as it is happening. The length of time it takes to transport goods and people to a different location has been reduced from weeks to days (even hours). It has become impossible for any nation to remain isolated. Every developed country has experienced twin problems: rapidly rising health care costs and a sluggish or failing economy.

Since the twenty-first century began, health care providers have been facing the following factors:

— Consumer movements (protection of patient rights, informed consent, reporting, privacy)

— Managed care (prepaid health care, reshaped health care)

— Increased use of ambulatory centers (may be stand-alone centers)

— Integration of health care organisations, departments within the organisations

— Health maintenance organisations (HMOs)

— The aging of the population

Changes in Delivery of Care

Other changes in the delivery of care have been labelled clinical pathways, empowering, restructuring, cross-functional training, decentralisation, care paths, interdisciplinary team approach, and integrated systems approach. Regardless of the labels placed on these changes, all of these approaches have some of the following commonality:

— Flattening of organisational structure, from the familiar pyramid-shaped organisation with six or more levels of management to a structure with just three or four levels may not be necessary
— Redesigning of technological content and services
— Improvement of the admission and discharge procedures
— Training people to do more than one function
— Reducing the lengths of stay
— Maintaining a stable, fiscally viable organisation
— Building high-performance teams that empower personnel to do their jobs and take necessary risks
— Implementing standards and rewards to give control of care back to patients
— Benchmarking internally and with competitors

Political and Government Intervention

The future direction of health care will be influenced by political and governmental intervention as a direct result of increased public awareness and demands. Regulation of the health care industry is likely to continue, even intensify, as access to care becomes a concern of politicians and consumers alike. Health care food service departments will feel the effects of the political environment as it shapes and regulates the way service is delivered. In addition to regulation, managers will see the effects of more emphasis on environmental safety while they struggle to provide accurate nutrition information to consumers.

In U.S.A. the regulations that currently have the greatest effect on health care are those dictated by Medicare and Medicaid, the largest managed care providers in the United States. Reimbursement rates for services have been set by Medicare and embraced by other managed care systems. Although most food service managers recognise their responsibility to provide a high-quality and safe food delivery system, Medicare regulations continue to ensure these entitlements for consumers. Medicare regulations affect the nutrition services offered, those services for which a fee is charged, and the quality of care delivered through meal service. Emphasis is on adherence to medically approved diets, written prescriptions, and the service of wholesome food. Medicaid coverage continues to be an ongoing problem, with various bills awaiting action in both the House and the Senate. By 2012 Medicare spending will exceed $425 billion, with 69.3 million beneficiaries.

Medicare budgets will increase more than 44 percent. Medicaid is the largest and fastest growing part of the state budgets, comprising 20 percent of all state expenditures. The number is expected to grow as the population ages, the need for long-term care increases, and older people enter nursing homes. Medicaid is the largest purchaser of nursing home services and maternity care in the nation. Much of the anticipated increase in spending will go to purchasing prescription drugs.

Food service departments that serve hospital extended-care units and long-term care facilities also must comply with the Medicare and Medicaid Requirements for Long-Term Care Facilities. These requirements, finalised in September 1992, implement the nursing home reform amendments enacted by the Omnibus Budget Reconciliation Act (OBRA) of 1987, as published by the Health Care Financing Administration. It is estimated that nearly 50 percent of the OBRA regulations relate directly or indirectly to nutrition and food service departments. The OBRA standards pertain to dignity and independence in dining, initial and annual nutrition assessments, nutrition care plans, and participation of a dietitian in family conferences.

Medicare and Medicaid regulations are government imposed, but some facilities choose to further their compliance efforts by following standards set by independent organisations. The JCAHO is one such organisation. Standards set by the JCAHO are similar to those set by Medicare; however, JCAHO surveys tend to place more emphasis on the systems, processes, and procedures that influence quality of patient care and outcomes. More recently, publications by the JCAHO report that future emphasis will be on the education and training of patients and their families; orientation, training, and education of staff; leadership roles of directors; and approaches and methods of quality improvement. They also have announced increased standards for safety, infection control, pain management, and emergency readiness. They will no longer announce the date or time of the surveys. Because JCAHO guidelines are updated and published annually, they must be reviewed annually to ensure compliance.

In addition to significantly influencing operations, legislation continues to dictate employment practices. As the labour force shrinks and alternative labour sources are explored, Americans with disabilities are one solution to some of the problems associated with inadequate staffing. Furthermore, ensuring equal employment opportunities for this segment of the population is mandated by federal law.

In 1990, President George H. W. Bush signed the Americans with Disabilities Act, which prohibits employment discrimination against the disabled. The act mandated that employers with 25 or more employees are prohibited from discriminating against qualified individuals with disabilities with regard to applications, hiring, discharge, compensation, advancement, training, or other terms, conditions, or privileges of employment. The act affects both the selection of employees and the service of meals to consumers.

Increasing Health Care Cost

Given the alarming rate of increase in health care costs and in an aging population, alternative health care options will be necessary. It is estimated that by 2011 the total national health expenditures will be $2,815,813 and will account for 17 percent of the gross domestic product. By 2009 the percentage of uninsured workers will be between 22 and 30 percent or about 60 million workers by 2011. The American Hospital Association (AHA) has called for hospital leaders to become active in reforming the health care delivery system. Specifically, the AHA has developed a model that calls for health care organisations to integrate care and collaborate to form networks at the community level. Community networking would prevent the duplication of services and thereby lower cost. Through assessment of community needs and consolidation of services, access to care also can be expanded to the uninsured. More health care institutions will move toward a seamless delivery of service and evolve into acute care facilities, with extended-care, home care, and ambulatory care facilities becoming majority caregivers.

The concept of seamless delivery of care is demonstrated by hospital-based, long-term care beds, with patients being moved to skilled-nursing beds or rehabilitation units designed to assist them in becoming self-sufficient. Moving from the higher-cost acute care setting benefits patients, hospitals, and payers. Meals and menus continue to increase in complexity (such as the introduction of the "spoken menu" and the computer-ordered menu) and diversity to meet the needs of inpatients in skilled-nursing and rehabilitation units. Although hospitals continue to convert unused beds to long-term care beds, most growth in long-term care is occurring in outside facilities. The elderly population, aged 85 years and older, will be about 17.6 million in 2050, with about 66 percent of this number being women. Assisted living continues to increase as more facilities become available.

Extended-care facilities are becoming more innovative in meeting their patients' mealtime needs. Many such facilities now provide selective menus; others have experimented with wait service and restaurant-style menus (that is, a number of selections per category per meal). Providing meals that meet the required nutrition modifications for elderly patients is becoming easier with the use of general diets that are lower in fat, sodium, and sugar; the liberalisation of other diets; and the increased number of products on the market that meet texture adjustment needs.

Services for Home

Patients' lengths of stay vary from one institution to another and from one geographical region to another. The average length of stay is affected by the high acuity level of patients. The high acuity level of a patient determines the need for extended care after discharge. Home care is one type of extended care that can positively influence the cost of health care, allowing for shorter hospital stays while ensuring that a patient is cared for in a familiar setting. Furthermore, readmissions have been shown to decrease as a result of team-managed home care. Advances in technology allow more services to be performed in the home, including infusion therapy (such as total parenteral nutrition). Home care offers bigger challenges for home delivery of meals, as does the continuing decline in funding for meal programs for the elderly.

Ambulatory care is expected to show significant growth throughout the next decade. The number of outpatient procedures continues to increase, resulting in a net increase in adjusted admissions. Surgical procedures in ambulatory care settings continue to increase nationwide. Technological advancements and reimbursement trends continue to support the shift from inpatient services to outpatient services. Emergency department visits increased due to a larger number of individuals without health insurance and the enforcement of the federal Emergency Medical Treatment and Labour Act. Outpatient visits will continue to increase by a rate of 15.7 percent per year. Even though hospital food service departments continue to encounter declines in the number of meal demands for inpatients, the number of meals prepared for nonpatients is likely to increase. For example, as outpatient procedures increase, food service departments will serve more visitors and family members who accompany patients as well as employees associated with ambulatory care.

Case Management and Patient-Focused Care

The goals of case management and patient-focused (or patient-centered) care are to improve patient care and satisfaction, decrease the cost of delivery, and improve access to health care. Patient-centered care is a more advanced extension of case management, but both are designed to use critical pathways or standardised care paths that specify a "road map" for the care team and are specific to individual diagnoses. The standards of care or critical paths, developed with input from all team members, are based on the best-demonstrated practice within the facility. Comparing the standards and paths with those at other organisations can help further quality improvement efforts. The patient-focused care model uses a case manager or coordinator who is assigned to a patient on admission and is responsible for monitoring the patient's progress throughout the hospital stay.

Patient-centered care eliminates traditional departmental lines, opting instead for health care teams that focus on patients with related conditions. To realise this type of care, a change in employee attitudes and structural changes to patient care units are necessary. Changes in these units will affect the nutrition and food service department as well as clinical caregivers. In models across the nation, food service workers are cross-trained to deliver meals and assist patients with their other needs. Some models assimilate jobs previously done by food service staff, housekeeping staff, and nurses' aides into new positions, such as the multiskilled patient care employee.

In addition to health care affordability, health care access has become a national priority in public calls for health care reform. The number of underinsured or uninsured persons will continue to rise as unemployment increases. Indigent care will continue to be a major issue as society's demographics change and the number of individuals living at or below the poverty level rises. Access to care will be coupled with equal quality for all, meaning that a uniform standard of care will continue to be a regulatory focus. The question confronting health care reform advocates is: Will universal access apply to only basic services or to all services?

Some health care institutions have begun to meet the needs of indigent persons through mobile clinics designed to deliver basic health services. Caring for these individuals will likely require participation from nutrition and food service personnel through the provision of either meals or clinical services such as nutritional assessment and counselling. Access to care is connected to questions on ethical decision making. Because today's health care system is ill equipped to provide equal care to the entire population, reforms must address what services should be universally accessible versus those limited to individuals capable of paying. Whereas the general population may recognise the restrictions of providing complete care for all, the context changes when the choice must be made for an individual or for loved ones.

Ethics in Clinical Care

Ethics play a role for nutrition and food service managers in their decisions regarding meal delivery and clinical care. For example, purchasers of food and supplies must avoid suppliers whose offer of favours or gifts would place them in a compromising purchasing position. As part of the health care team, registered dietitians must give input regarding the delivery of nutrition hydration services to terminally ill patients. Some ethical issues dealing with nutrition management are addressed by state-specific advance directives signed when patients are admitted to a facility. These advance directives, which reflect a patient's wishes, help physicians and other caregivers in their decisions about the course of treatment.

In 1990, the Environmental Protection Agency reported that the amount of waste being sent to landfills had decreased to 67 percent, down from 80 percent in 1988. Even so, Americans continue to generate more waste than ever before. Each individual generates about five tons of waste per year. If this rate of growth continues, many landfills will be closed and there will be a demand for new ones or for shipping the waste to offshore locations.

Health care and food service, both separately and together, have been targets in the environmental controversy. The waste from food service operations is composed of 60 percent to 70 percent of solid waste that includes food, paper, and plastic supplies such as napkins and single-use plastic items. The remaining 30 percent to 40 percent is from food production and preparation. Waste management efforts in all areas of health care should consider three agendas: reducing the quantity of waste, reusing as many materials or items as possible, and recycling used materials. The increase in environmental regulation and public concern is forcing health care institutions to take innovative measures in handling medical waste, which includes many hazardous products as well as infectious waste that usually is incinerated.

Many food service opportunities exist to decrease waste and to implement recycling systems. For example, using individual coffee mugs and soft drink cups and eliminating or limiting disposable tableware can reduce waste. Recycling office paper, glass, steel and aluminum cans, and corrugated paper is another waste-reduction effort. Many health care organisations have found a way to simultaneously decrease landfill use and help those less fortunate. For example, programs designed to feed the hungry are operated in many metropolitan areas.

Food products prepared by health care food service departments are picked up by volunteers and distributed to organisations that distribute the food to homeless or low-income individuals. These programs have an added advantage in that the food service manager can measure and monitor food waste so as to improve preparation forecasts.

In 1992, the Food and Drug Administration (FDA) announced food-labelling regulations in conjunction with the Nutrition Labelling and Education Act of 1990. Both the number of foods covered and the amount of information required on labels have increased. The purpose of this legislation and ensuing regulation is to provide consumers with more reliable and informative material. Since May 1994, all processed foods regulated by the FDA must be appropriately labelled, and labels must include standardised serving sizes, grams of saturated fat, and fibre content.

The percentage of daily values provides the percentage of fat, saturated fat, cholesterol, sodium, carbohydrate, and fibre contributed by a single serving, based on a 2,000-calorie daily diet. The new guidelines allow seven nutrient or disease-specific relationship claims and provide more detailed ingredient listings. Labels that use free, lean, lite, or extra lean must meet the established standards for these product descriptions. An exemption to providing nutrition labels has been made for food served for immediate consumption, unless health claims are made. This exemption applies to restaurants and health care food service facilities.

However, if health claims are made, these facilities have to meet the specific guidelines for the nutrient, and the claims must be verified by a minimum of three chemical analyses. For example, a claim that a product is low in cholesterol requires that the product have three verification analyses that prove it is at least 30 percent lower than the original product. Foods that are organically grown and irradiated foods must be labelled as such. Companies that wish to include genetically enhanced ingredients in their food products may label genetically enhanced ingredients and ingredients enhanced using biotechnology.

Impact of Globalisation

Globalisation, deregulation, and technology are changing the nature of jobs and work. Today over two-thirds of the

U.S. workforce is employed in producing services, not products. Of 21 million new jobs added through the 1990s, many will become part-time, and virtually all will be in service industries such as food service, retailing, consulting, teaching, and legal work. The civilian workforce is expected to grow by 17 million people by 2010, reaching about 158 million. The demand for institutional food service jobs such as chefs, cooks, and dietitians is expected to be the highest. Because of the increased number of dual-income families and women, who make up 48 percent of the workforce, and because of the aging of baby boomers, the demand for service workers has grown.

Food service managers in health care will have to compete with other service industries for the dwindling labour resources. A reduction in skilled workers coupled with an increased need for food service workers will require higher pay scales, which will negatively affect budget and cost-control efforts. Not only has the labour market diminished, the demographics have changed: The workforce of the next decade will be older, more culturally diverse, and include more women, people with disabilities, and those with sexual or affectional orientation.

These trends will continue, especially with the increasing diversity of the population. The decrease in the number of teenaged workers and the increase in the number of workers older than 50 changes the face of the average employee. Baby boomers will still be in the workforce before becoming eligible for Medicare. As a result, the largest pool of workers will also be the older labour force, with the number of workers aged 55 to 65 increasing to about 8.5 million. According to the Bureau of Labour Statistics (BLS), the median age of the labour force will continue to rise, even though the rate of growth in the youth labour force (16 to 24 years old) is expected to be larger than the growth rate for the overall labour force.

The growth rate for the female labour force is expected to slow, but it will grow more rapidly than the male labour force. By 2010, the workforce will comprise 52 percent men and 48 percent women. As mentioned earlier, the full effects of the Americans with Disabilities Act have yet to be felt but are expected to be tied closely with the aging of the population, escalation of the acquired immunodeficiency syndrome (AIDS) epidemic, and job shortage. The decreasing literacy rate among the nation's workers continues to be an area of focus. A shrinking labour pool necessitates identifying employees as customers and focusing on their needs.

Health care nutrition and food service departments represent entry points where training becomes more of a priority. Employee socialisation and retention are specific concerns for food service directors. The number of younger women (ages 25 to 29) entering the workforce continues to increase but at a substantially lower rate than before 1985. A slower economy and an escalation in the number of births for this age group are cited by the BLS as a reason for the slowdown. Incentives-benefits, flexible schedules, job sharing, maternity leave, and child care centers-will need to be provided for them to return to work.

Workers aged 50 years and older are expected to remain the dominant age group during the remainder of the next decade. The aging of the workforce has been attributed to maturing of the baby boomers, lower birthrates, and increased life expectancy. The shrinking pool of available workers and the growing number of older workers has necessitated their selection as alternative labour. Today's older worker is healthier and can work longer than the same-age worker of a few decades ago. Having knowledge of the average worker's age and the diversity of the labour force helps food service managers make the changes needed to attract and retain employees. The value system of most of the workforce will be based on worker individuality, maximum amount and control of free time away from work, and participation in deciding how work is accomplished. These values will require nutrition and food service managers to be flexible with schedules, including total hours worked, workdays, and responsibilities.

Closely tied to the Americans with Disabilities Act is the treatment of employees with AIDS in the workplace. In terms of knives and other tools and equipment that could cause cuts, certain risks are involved with kitchen employees who are HIV positive. Closely tied to AIDS-and perhaps more important to food service managers-is the near-epidemic number of cases of TB currently identified. Because TB is an airborne infection that is highly contagious, food service managers have to diligently ensure annual employee physical examinations.

About 2.5 million or more Americans who are illiterate are expected to enter the workforce each year; many will be attracted to the service industry, specifically food service. Of about 69 percent of Americans who finish high school, only two-thirds will have adequate skills for employment. With the predictions of future labour shortages, quality of education and on-the-job training are increasingly important employment considerations. On-the-job training, once limited to specific job skills, has to go a step further to provide basic reading and writing skills. Partnerships between educational institutions and health care organisations are in demand to improve the knowledge base of the fewer number of entry-level employees available for food service work. Some organisations now include basic literacy courses as part of the health care employee-training program intended to provide service areas with needed staff.

The leaders of today and tomorrow have to consider employees not only as a resource but also as a valuable asset to be empowered, trained, and properly motivated. Although expert predictions that the demands of tomorrow's workforce will be linked to autonomy, more time off, and their being included in decisions affecting their work may hold some truth, differing employee value systems must be considered as a factor in this scenario. Value systems vary from one individual to another based on age, culture, and past experiences.

Awareness of Nutrition

Today's consumers have an increased awareness of nutrition and the effect diet can have on their health. Nutrition information collected through research efforts is no longer the exclusive domain of professionals who pass this information on to their patients. Consumers are bombarded at every turn with reports on the latest nutrition research through television, newspapers, magazines, and numerous books and pamphlets. Although intended to educate consumers, this information is often conflicting and not easily interpreted for application to daily dietary intake. Because informed consumers are not always wiser consumers, attempts must be made to meet their perceived needs if customer satisfaction is the goal.

Heightened nutrition awareness is closely linked with an increased emphasis on fitness. Yesterday's fitness fad is today's lifestyle for many consumers of health care and nutrition and food service. Even so, people continue to indulge their appetites, especially when dining out. The number one health problem is now obesity. Portions in fast-food outlets, restaurants, and other food service operations continue to be "supersize," adding additional unneeded calories. Increased nutrition awareness and health education will prove beneficial for patients who desire to participate actively in their care. This trend may be one answer to lowering the cost of delivering health care while improving customer satisfaction.

In contrast, the large number of less knowledgeable persons living at or below the poverty level will be further disadvantaged by the continued economic dual tiering of society and the growth of a minority immigrant population. The upward trend of poverty will negatively affect the number of individuals at nutritional risk in communities and further validate the role of nutrition awareness.

Demographic Changes in Food Services and Health Care

Three primary demographic changes will affect the delivery of nutrition and food services in health care: an aging population, more women as decision makers, and cultural diversity. By 2010 the median age will be 37.4 years, and by far the largest age group will be younger than 19 years. Their health care needs will continue to center on preventive medicine, fitness, nutrition, and well-child checkups. In addition, this age group will become the primary caregivers for the majority segment-the elderly. Those from age 60 to 80 and older will be the largest segment of the population.

Aging Population

The aging of the population, or the graying of America, is reflected in an increased acuity level of patients, an increased number of patients at nutritional risk, and more older patients requiring health care than at any other time in history. The fastest-growing population segment includes those older than 50, who represent 30 percent of the population. By 2010, the U.S. Census Bureau projects that 21 million Americans will be between the ages of 65 and 74, a 15 percent increase over 1989. This shift is fostering extensive growth in extended-care facilities, including nursing homes, adult day care centers, and retirement centers.

In addition to the increased growth in these freestanding facilities, a larger number of hospitals include skilled-nursing units and rehabilitation units. In addition to caring for the elderly once they become ill, health care organisations are proactively designing preventive care programs to evaluate the health needs of older persons and provide appropriate education. Evaluation includes individualised screens for nutritional risk and guidelines for improving nutrition status related to illness prevention and treatment.

Women's Role in Decision Making

Women are the primary decision makers in health care delivery choices and want more involvement in matters dealing with their health and that of their families. Centers and specific departments that consider their unique needs continue to influence the delivery of care. Interest in women's health concerns also is evidenced by increased research in this area. As the average life expectancy continues to increase, women are facing more responsibility in caring for parents and other extended family members as well as their immediate families. This fact, together with the expanding number of women entering the workforce, will further emphasise customer satisfaction from the perspective of women. As health care decision makers, women influence the balance between high-touch and high-tech aspects of care.

In addition to those nutrition and food service demands already mentioned-affordability, continuity of care, equal access, and so forth-the growing number of working women expect convenience. Food choices for this group are influenced by the makeup of the family unit, and many experts in nutrition and food service predict that children will become the new "gatekeepers" of the food supply. Convenient, well-prepared, nutritious food becomes a key element in this scenario as the demands of female consumers provide opportunities for health care food service managers. For example, the cafeteria can be extended to offer take-out services, bakery products, and prepackaged kids' meals.

Cultural Diversity

The effects of cultural diversity on food service are prominently reflected in menus enhanced with ethnic dishes. Some operators call for a return to more basic, home-style "American" food choices, but the question arises as to what that means. For example, one of the most popular foods in America is pizza, followed closely by Mexican and Asian food selections. These cuisines have become American menu staples. In planning menus, food service managers should consider the population to be served. Demographics vary by region in age and cultural diversity and should be evaluated before making menu selections. Although menus may return to basics in the coming decade and reflect lighter fare, the signature items of various cultures will find a place.

Growth of Technology

The past several decades have been marked by a pronounced growth in technology. The area that underwent the most rapid growth was information services. In general, health care has been slow to implement computerisation, especially in food service. Many hospitals today, however, have chief information officers who coordinate computer systems planning and implementation. In addition to information technology, medical technology has significantly changed the delivery of health care.

Both diagnostic advances and treatment technology have improved patient outcomes while placing extreme financial burdens on health care organisations. Because of heavy diagnostic and clinical advances, many nutrition and food service departments have been left out of the capital expenditure cycle or have spent more time justifying equipment needs. However, this does not mean that significant advances have not been made in food service technology that are important to the delivery of cost-effective, high-quality food service.

Implementing Information Systems

Information systems will continue to dominate the technological front in the coming decades. Information systems in health care organisations over the past decade have been primarily in the areas of financial, accounting, and human resource management. This emphasis will continue and become more refined in assisting management with making budget-related decisions and with reporting specific information for the new requirements established by Medicare and Medicaid.

Current emphasis is on the design and implementation of a universal electronic data interchange system for processing health care claims. This system necessitates the development of a common language for hospitals, the federal government, and insurers, along with standardisation of core financial information. Most hospital billing departments do not find it easy to accommodate a common language or method because of the lack of integration of computer systems and the large volume of services billed. This type of common claims processing will make it increasingly necessary for hospitals to improve their current computer systems. Medical professionals are including clinical information systems in their office practices.

Much of this technology provides for more accurate diagnosis, improved customer care, and improved patient medical records. As the technology becomes more commonplace, future professionals will have greater access and comfort levels. Clinical information systems tie diagnostic testing results directly to nurses' station or physicians' offices, a linkage that allows quick review and action on test results and facilitates improved patient care. Bedside charting, a term used more and more frequently in discussions of patient care, and the computerised medical record improve information flow, thereby assisting with reimbursement. Information systems also are important in the food service department, where management control systems are numerous and their applications vary considerably.

Systems may include software packages designed to manage information for clinical management and meal service; menu planning; forecasting and purchasing; inventory management; food safety; payroll; financial management; and in skilled-nursing facilities, material data sheets. Many vendors or distributors offer food service operators a direct computer link to warehouses for the purpose of placing orders and accessing information regarding purchase history. Food service inventory systems range from department-specific personal computers and software to mainframe systems designed for the organisation. Information is entered into inventory either manually or through the use of a scanner.

Still other software programs include nutrition analysis and additional clinical applications. As it becomes increasingly important to evaluate past and current information to make the best decisions for tomorrow, advanced information systems will become more significant. The use of computer systems may not decrease staff needs, but in today's environment they are necessary to manage the increasing amount of information needed by managers to run their departments effectively. Computer software should be purchased based on individual needs.

The delivery of high-quality health care continues to rely on technology, the increased cost of which tends to affect health care faster than other businesses. This cost dynamic is due to rapid changes in technology that can be linked to equipment obsolescence over a short time period, acquisition or replacement costs, and the effects of competition among facilities. Some technological advances have been able to reduce labour needs, but more have required new or higher skill levels. A more demanding skill requirement has led to specialisation within departments or fields, making it difficult to use staff for a variety of tasks. Technology also can be effective not only in diagnostics but also in treatment to lower costs and decrease the length of stay.

Technology has been responsible for decreasing patient admissions and for increasing the use of outpatient services. More general surgery is being performed as laparoscopic surgery, which can be done in the outpatient setting. Another type of medical technology with widespread effects on health care involves pharmaceuticals. The number of new medications entering the marketplace yearly is staggering. The rapid pace of development creates new problems for the FDA and for the public in that a number of medications have been recalled after their extended use was found to cause side effects not predicted in trials before FDA approval. In view of the AIDS crisis, for instance, demands for rapid approval and release of pharmaceuticals are not likely to decrease.

Food Technology

This technology is proving to be the least controversial and most widely accepted by both food service professionals and customers. Because many of the products prepared and preserved with low-temperature cooking and vacuum sealing are considered gourmet in nature, food service managers can expand and improve menu options for patients and other customer groups. Biotechnology is creating the taste of the future. In this form of genetic engineering, a gene foreign to a product is spliced or added to its DNA to enhance or inhibit qualities of the original product. This bioengineering technology is being used to improve the current food supply; for example, vegetables and fruits are engineered to resist spoilage, increase variety, improve nutritional content, enhance resistance to disease and freezing, and provide a longer shelf life. The major reason for pursuing these genetically altered products is to decrease the amount of chemicals used during growing; by altering certain genes, the plants can be made resistant to insects.

Advantages of new equipments

Advantages in equipment should be considered annually when making capital equipment plans. Equipment needs vary from one institution to another and depend on the types of food purchased, the production methods used, staffing, and the menu. Recent advances in food service equipment include cook-and-chill units, microwaves, blast chillers, and smaller versions of existing equipment. Cook-and-chill units have been used in Europe since the 1960s but were not in widespread use in the United States until the 1980s. Their use is important in institutional food service, as operators strive to serve high-quality products assisted by a dwindling skilled labour force.

Food is prepared using standard cooking methods with some modification of starch for some items and then chilled rapidly in a blast chiller for later use. Some managers have also advocated the use of blast chillers to ensure safe cooling of bulk products before storage so as to prevent spoilage. The cook-and-chill method can be used with standard production techniques, when food is prepared for one day's service, placed in serving pans and chilled, and then used to plate meals cold for rethermalisation. Cook-and-chill systems also can be complex, requiring the purchase of other equipment such as cook tanks, specially designed pumps, and rethermalisation units.

Many smaller versions of ovens and other equipment on the market were developed in response to limitations on space and the desire of some operators to use equipment in the view of customers. Other operators have installed preparation equipment-for example, a pizza oven-in full view of their customers. Microwaves, once used for boiling water or reheating foods, are finding their way into preparation areas of many food service departments. Microwaves can be used to reheat the many frozen products on the market and are excellent for preparing vegetables.

Another equipment advancement is robotics, computerised units that assist with repetitive motion, such as placing items on patients' trays and cooking hamburgers. Technology is available to fully automate many kitchen and service activities. Equipment designs no doubt will consider changes in tomorrow's labour force. Instructions must be clear and understandable to workers whose abilities to read English may be limited, and knobs or switches must be designed for physically challenged individuals.

Today food is served in homes; restaurants; schools; colleges; universities; health care organisations; the military; corrections facilities; clubs and other social organisations; day care centers; and industrial, business, and transportation enterprises. Each of the facilities plan, price their menus, and provide a variety of eating rooms, from elegant dining to tray service in health care to fast food that may be eaten in an automobile.

The food service industry is one of the world's largest businesses, with a sales volume of about $400 billion. Food service is also the number one employer among all retail businesses, with more than 11 million persons employed, most being women and about 25 percent being teenagers. According to the BLS, food service and preparation jobs are the fastest-growing national occupation. It is predicted that it will continue to increase. The BLS also predicts a shortage of registered dietitians in the next decade.

There are 844,000 food service operations in the United States. Many U.S. households continuously rely on others for their food preparation. By the year 2010, more than half of every consumer food dollar will be spent on food service rather than groceries. Restaurants account for 62 percent of food service sales. Elder care is the fastest-growing market; correctional food service continues to grow and is expected to have a rapid growth in the next few years, with the greatest increase in federal prisons. More than 10 million meals per year come from correctional facilities.

Health care institutions, like many of the noncommercial food service operations, serve a captive audience. Their budgets for expense are included in the hospital room rate, and many health care food services are subsidised, which means they receive some funds from external sources.

The food service industry is made up of a broad scope of establishments. These establishments are classified as commercial, noncommercial, and institutional. Commercial food service has as its primary activity the preparation and service of food. In noncommercial and institutional food service, the preparation and service of food is a secondary activity. The commercial segment includes fast-food, quick-service, or limited-menu restaurants; fine-dining restaurants; airport restaurants; convenience stores; buffet and self-serve restaurants; catering; supermarkets; food courts; and retail outlets such as department stores. These establishments set their own menu, price structure, and hours of service. Some, like airport restaurants, may serve the same customer only once or twice a year.

The noncommercial segment, where entities operate their own food service, includes hotel and motel restaurants, country club restaurants, cruise ships, trains, airlines, zoos, sporting events, and theme parks. Each of these establishments may depend on the economy. When the economy is good, customers tend to spend more money to indulge in eating in these restaurants. The institutional segment includes the military; correctional facilities; hospitals; child care centers; senior care facilities; extended-care facilities such as nursing homes and other health care centers; employee food service for offices, industrial complexes, and health care facilities; schools, colleges, and universities; and not-for-profit establishments.

All of the institutional segments have several things in common: a captive audience; low cost per meal; many regulatory agencies' standards; and local, state, and federal government regulations that must be met. In-house management of noncommercial institutional food service has remained steady over the past decade. Many noncommercial operations hire contract food service organisations that manage the food service department as well as other departments. Contract food service management is the provision of food service by a third-party company through a contract. The company meets the objectives of the department but is profit oriented. The contract company provides management of the food service operation for the organisation and in some instances may also provide clinical services.

Some organisations may outsource some of their services, such as information services or purchasing. Outsourcing means that an outside company will provide a service that the organisation may not have the staff or equipment to do on-site. Self-operation is the opposite of contract management. Self-operating food service is defined as the organisation or institution being responsible for the management and clinical components of food service. There is an ongoing discussion of the advantages and disadvantages of contract management versus self-operation.

Food Service in Health Care Organisation

The role of food service in a health care organisation is to provide a variety of food that is nutritious and well-prepared in a safe and sanitary environment that meets the financial obligation of the department while meeting the needs of customers and is served in a pleasing and attractive manner. The department will strive to meet the social, cultural, religious, and psychological needs of customers in meal planning and service. The staff provides education to its customers while they are patients in the health care facility, in outpatient consultations, in the community, and to the general public, as requested.

Workers in the food service department are leaders within the organisation who adhere to the overall mission, vision, and values of the organisation while dovetailing the department's mission, vision, and values to those of the organisation. The role of the food service is to develop goals and outcome objectives and to seek commitment to achieving the outcomes. The department works with other departments within the organisation in a team effort to provide for customers. The largest challenge to face a food service department is to provide food to its customers while integrating the department's activities into the overall operation of the organisation.

Food service directors face ethical challenges and social responsibility as they balance the organisation's need to know and the privacy requests of employees and cultural and ethical behaviours of a diverse workforce and customer base to ensure that the organisation is working in a socially responsible manner. Ethics is defined as the principles of conduct governing an individual or business or the views, attitudes, and practices about what is right or wrong; it concerns moral standards and basic values. There are professional or business and personal ethics.

Organisations such as the American Dietetic Association and the Dietary Managers Association have written codes of ethics that are guidelines for members of the organisation. These codes are to promote and maintain the highest standards of food and nutrition services and personal contact among its members. Some organisations have a bill of rights for employees that assists managers in dealing with employees while ensuring the rights of employees.

13

EMERGENCY FOOD SERVICES

Every year natural and man-made disasters afflict numerous communities. In large-scale disasters, human needs are so great and social disorganisation is so widespread that regular community social services are unable to cope. Only emergency social services response systems can meet urgent physical and personal needs until longer-term programmes are established. Like in U.S.A., Emergency Social Services (ESS) is a planned emergency response organisation designed to provide disaster victims with essential services. The concept of ESS is not present in developing countries like India whereas in developed countries like U.S.A. have a full time organised Emergency Social Services. The ESS has five service components:

— *Emergency Clothing Service*: supplies clothing or emergency covering until regular sources of supply are available.

— *Emergency Lodging Service*: arranges for safe, temporary lodging for homeless or evacuated people.

— *Emergency Food Service*: feeds evacuees, emergency workers, and disaster volunteers.

— *Registration and Inquiry Service*: attempts to reunite families by collecting information and answering queries about missing persons.

— *Personal Services*: receives disaster victims at reception centres; provides information about emergency help; offers temporary care for unattended children and dependent, elderly women and men; helps provide temporary care for residents of special care facilities; offers immediate and long-term emotional support, where needed.

Relevant government agencies and community organisations undertake to develop local ESS plans. Participants may include:

— municipal or provincial departments of social services, public health, mental health, family and children's services, etc.

— private social service agencies.

— service clubs, church groups, branches of national organisations; and

— business and professional associations.

A community's ESS response organisation is generated by and integrally linked to existing human service organisations. It supports the existing human services structure, and does not replace it. The community plan outlines emergency roles of municipal police, fire, transport and social service departments, plus major utilities, ambulance companies, and others. The ESS response plan is part of the overall community response plan and should be developed in conjunction with the community plan.

Emergency Food Service (EFS)

In times of disaster, food is essential to sustain life, counteract shock, raise the morale of evacuees and provide energy for workers labouring under stressful conditions. An Emergency Food Service is an emergency response organisation designed to provide food for:

— those who cannot feed themselves, or those without food or food preparation facilities; and

— recovery workers and volunteers

To be effective, Emergency Food Service programmes must be able to:

— help evacuees cope with a disaster by meeting their needs for a sufficient amount of food to maintain a feeling of well-being;

— meet the special food requirements of high-risk groups, including infants, children, pregnant and nursing women, the elderly, diabetics, and disaster workers;

— provide appropriate food service.

Essential considerations include:

— food requirements (hot or cold meals; quantities)

— available supplies, staff and facilities

— the time of year (i.e. winter, summer)

— religious or cultural requirements

— the need for safe, wholesome food

Organisation of Food Service (FS)

To respond rapidly to the nutritional needs of disaster evacuees, communities need well trained FS organisations which can begin operating as soon as a disaster strikes.

A community's size dictates the structure and scope of an FS organisation. The organisation should be flexible enough to respond to a variety of emergency situations and demands. To ensure a prompt and effective emergency response, FS staff must clearly understand their roles and responsibilities.

Role of FS Chief

The Director of Emergency Social Services appoints and trains the FS Chief. He or she is responsible for advance preparations as well as emergency responses and post-emergency measures. Prior to a disaster, the FS Chief:

— selects an FS planning and organising committee;

— establishes good working relations with food retailers, wholesalers, and distributors;

— develops an FS response plan;

— selects and trains staff;

— tests the plan by conducting regular FS exercises, then revises and updates the plan;

— co-ordinates the FS plan with the four other ESS plans;

— notifies the Director of ESS about a building suitable for the FS, and

— makes certain that all FS operational sites have adequate equipment and supplies.

During a disaster, the FS Chief:

— reports to the ESS co-ordination centre and, if required, initiates and directs FS operations;

— ensures the maintenance of an FS log and provides ongoing reports on problems, needs, and activities to the Director of ESS, and

— co-ordinates food supplies, including distribution to reception centres.

After a disaster, the FS Chief:

— makes certain that FS staff are included in a stress-debriefing session, and

— prepares a post-disaster report on FS emergency activities for the Director of ESS.

The FS Planning Committee helps the FS Chief prepare detailed Food Service plans.

Recruit FS planning committee members from the community. Suitable participants include:

— restaurateurs, hotel and canteen managers;
— dietitians, food technicians, home economists, nutritionists, and chefs;
— supervisors of commercial cafeterias;
— volunteer representatives of the Canadian Red Cross, the Salvation Army, Meals on Wheels and other community meal distribution programmes; and
— public health officials, food caterers, food retailers, wholesalers, and distributors.

The planning committee helps the FS Chief to:

— secure the active participation of relevant food agencies and groups in the community;
— develop the FS response plan;
— identify immediate and ongoing food problems which disaster victims are likely to face;
— evaluate the availability of FS resources in the community, including personnel, supplies, and equipment, and
— assign FS response roles and responsibilities.

Role of Food Supervisors

The Chief of FS appoints a Food Supervisor for each designated reception centre in the community. The FS supervisor reports to the reception centre manager on administrative matters and to the FS Chief at the ESS headquarters on the operation of the FS. The Food Supervisor will:

— direct operations at the reception centres;
— mobilise staff when the FS plan goes into effect, and set up an FS in the reception centre;
— train FS staff at the designated reception centre;
— prepare work schedules;

— maintain nutritional variety;
— maintain proper sanitation practices and safe working conditions;
— keep an up-to-date log on borrowed items, messages and donations.
— report problems, needs and the status of activities to the FS Chief on a regular basis;
— keep in touch with other reception centres, and
— when the emergency is over, submit a report to the FS Chief and help evaluate the FS.

Role of FS Workers

The Food Supervisor supervises FS workers, including a chef, cooks, assistant cooks, and food servers. The Chef:
— prepares the menu to meet basic nutritional requirements with available supplies;
— organises the kitchen to ensure maximum efficiency and safety;
— plans a work schedule;
— assigns and supervises work;
— ensures proper storage of food supplies;
— oversees efficient organisation of stock, and
— ensures proper sanitation and safety standards are practiced in cooking, food distribution, and food storage areas.

Role of Cooks

— prepare stipulated meals and deliver food to the service counter;
— ensure an adequate supply of hot water is available;
— prepare food for transportation (if necessary).

Role of Food Servers

— set up a service counter;
— set up garbage disposal units near cafeteria exits;
— set up self-service for cutlery, milk, sugar, and condiments;
— serve portions according to the chef's specifications;
— keep cooks informed of food requirements, to ensure adequate supplies;
— replenish food during the meal, and
— keep service counters clean.

As soon as the meal is over, food servers must:

— transfer leftover food to the kitchen and store food properly, and
— clean service counters.

Role of Dishwashers and cleaners

— set up a separate dishwashing area for dishes and serving equipment;
— maintain cleanliness in the area;
— remove garbage;
— wash and sterilise garbage containers, and
— wash floors.

Role of Back-Up Staff

In a major disaster, the FS may have to operate on a 24-hour basis. Back-up staff will be needed to replace initial response staff.

Staff Recruitment

Experienced food service personnel are well-suited to FS work since they:

— work regularly in community food facilities;
— serve large quantities of food;
— plan menus;
— are capable of preparing meals under emergency conditions, and
— apply sanitary and food safety regulations.

In some communities, representatives of such local groups as the Salvation Army, the Canadian Red Cross and Meals on Wheels may accept these responsibilities.

In selecting candidates for key FS positions, look for the following:

— practical knowledge and experience in the food service field;
— an ability to plan, organise, and direct;
— training in emergency planning;
— familiarity with community resources;
— an ability to work under stress;
— initiative and flexibility in emergency situations, and
— knowledge of a variety of cultural diets and food preferences.

Mobile Emergency Food Service Team

Each reception centre must be equipped to outfit at least one Mobile Emergency Food Service team. Three types of mobile units are available.

Mobile canteen

A truck, station wagon or jeep can be made into a mobile canteen with the addition of portable sections. A simple unit, the mobile canteen is equipped to serve food which has been prepared elsewhere. Replenish food and eating utensils frequently. Suggested equipment for a mobile canteen are:

— can opener
— eating utensils
— containers for food and liquids
— disposable plates, cups
— garbage cans
— insulated containers, etc.
— serving utensils
— sugar and salt shakers
— pitchers
— trays
— a folding table (for serving)
— a portable stove to keep hot food hot (over 60°C/ 140°F)

Mobile kitchen

The mobile kitchen consists of one or more vehicles equipped to serve but not prepare food. It carries its own water, food supplies, and fuel.

Emergency Food Resource Survey

Survey your community for information about available food. The resulting Food Resource Directory enables the FS to respond rapidly to emergency food needs in a disaster.

Planning the Survey

The FS Chief is responsible for planning the Food Resource Survey, but he or she can be assisted by members of the

FS planning committee. The FS Chief briefs survey workers on survey procedures and information needed. Notify survey participants in advance by describing the purpose of the survey in a form letter signed by the FS Chief.

Conducting the Survey

Survey food establishments to obtain precise information about sources of food in the community.

Formal advance arrangements should be made with all prospective food suppliers at both the local and regional levels.

- Producers generate food.
- Processors clean, sort, and prepare food for shipment.
- Wholesalers supply commercial food establishments.
- Retailers include cafeterias, coffee shops, fast-food outlets, grocery stores, restaurants, and supermarkets.

Food service facilities

Identify food service operations in schools, colleges (private and public), universities, government buildings, hotels, motels, special care facilities, and churches. These facilities are usually available for emergency use and likely have both food preparation staff and a stock of food.

Mobile canteens, field kitchens

Canvass the community for mobile canteens and field kitchens. These are practical and flexible methods of providing food to people at remote and inaccessible sites. Individuals who operate commercial food-vending trucks are ideally suited to running mobile canteens and food kitchens in an emergency.

Emergency Equipment and Supplies Survey

Find and record sources of kitchen equipment and supplies. Determine the location of reception centres, food distribution and cooking areas in selected operating facilities and record these locations in the FS plan. Survey restaurants, food caterers and food suppliers in the local area and keep a record of names, addresses and telephone numbers.

Written Agreements

Negotiate emergency provisioning with surveyed suppliers. Include compensation rates and methods of payment, where applicable, in written agreements. The written agreement must specify:

— the type of food the supplier will provide,

— how quickly the supplier will provide it, and

— how the supplier will transport the food.

Maps and Boundaries

Prepare FS maps showing the quickest routes to local suppliers. Maps should indicate the location of:

— all sources of fresh water (lakes, rivers, springs, reservoirs, etc.);

— local food suppliers, wholesalers and retailers, including food warehouses, packing plants, supermarkets, and food distribution points;

— waste disposal sites;

— food preparation and serving sites;

— principle supply routes, in addition to the quickest supply routes, and

— remote feeding sites.

Record Keeping

List food, equipment, and other financial expenditures on forms for the FS Chief.

Emergency Food Directory

List survey information in an FS Directory. Use the Directory to locate essential supplies in an emergency. Review the Directory at least once a year, and keep information up-to-date.

Operational Guidelines

General operational guidelines are:

- — Ensure the availability of safe drinkable water.
- — Have a variety of baby foods available at all times.
- — Prepare milk and cereals for infants.
- — Serve evacuees and workers a hot or cold beverage.
- — Provide muffins, doughnuts, cookies, juice, milk, etc.
- — Establish priorities that meet the food needs of pregnant women, nursing mothers, the elderly, and diabetics.
- — Serve a nutritious meal to workers and provide non-stimulating drinks such as fruit juice, water, and bouillon on a regular basis, especially if their work is physically demanding.
- — Maintain proper sanitation practices and safe working conditions.
- — Serve familiar food to evacuees.

Some specific operational guidelines are:

Importance of an Adequate, Safe Water Supply: Notify FS personnel if there are water problems. In areas where local water is considered unsafe, water should be purified.

Infants: Mothers may continue to nurse. Nursing formulas (such as Similac, SMA, Enfalac etc.) should also be available.

Infants and Young Children: Keep supplies of ready-to-eat infant cereals for infants six months of age and over.

Pregnant Women and Nursing Mothers: Pregnant women and nursing mothers have no special food requirements, but they must drink an extra litre (1 quart) of milk per day and eat one citrus fruit per day.

Guidelines for Sanitation

Food handlers must obey sanitation regulations to avoid health risks. The risk of contamination increases in emergency situations since food servers are often overworked and operating under unsatisfactory conditions. To ensure safe food handling, closely supervise:

— the water supply
— food-storage methods
— workers' personal hygiene
— food preparation and service
— waste disposal
— dishwashing and rinsing procedures
— kitchen sanitation.

Personal hygiene

Personal hygiene regulations are well known, but constant supervision is needed to ensure basic rules are followed. Food handlers must:

— wash hands before and during food preparation
— work on a clean surface
— use clean utensils

— wear a hairnet or a net for beards
— stay home when sick.

Food Contamination

Strict sanitary rules must be implemented to ensure that carefully-selected, uncontaminated food and water does not become contaminated during meal preparations. Food-borne illnesses can be avoided by following good food-handling practices.

Operational Procedures at Warehouses

Dry food storage

Under disaster conditions, storage facilities may not be ideal. It is particularly important to observe the following guidelines:

— keep the storage area as cool and dry as possible;
— eliminate rodents and insects;
— store foods on shelves to ensure proper air circulation and protect against dampness;
— discard spoiled food;
— note the date food arrives;
— utilise food in rotation, according to purchase dates, and
— destroy damaged canned goods.

Refrigerated storage

Refrigeration is vital during a disaster. Basic safeguards to follow include:

— avoid overcrowding—plan food storage for best use of space;

— potentially hazardous food should be cooked well and cooled quickly by refrigerating below 4°C (40°F). This applies to milk products, milk-based desserts, meat, fish and poultry;

— note when food was cooked;

— place cooked foods above raw foods, and

— regularly wash the interior of the refrigerator and all containers.

Improvised Refrigeration

You may have to improvise refrigeration in certain disaster situations. Options include a desert cooler and a reach-in-pit cooler.

OPERATIONAL PROCEDURES

The Emergency Food Service is probably the most complex component of the ESS. The EFS team should work closely with other services to ensure that food service facilities are adequately located and meet minimum food storage, preparation and service requirements.

Responsibilities of Food Supervisor

Initial preparation

1. Meet the reception centre manager.
2. Check FS space allotment.
3. Mobilise staff.

Evacuees arrive and work begins

1. Set up the supervisory office.
2. Start a log—record dates and times of arrival.

3. Brief FS personnel on:
   - the number of people expected
   - problem areas
   - unusual resource requirements.
4. Check whether the following are ready to be used:
   - Food-receiving area
   - Food storage area
   - Kitchen area
   - Dishwashing area
   - Refrigeration units
   - Garbage receptacles
   - Cafeteria
   - Service counters
   - Entrances
   - Exits
   - Traffic flow

Second priorities

1. Specify boundaries for food service coverage.
2. Check numbers to be fed at the reception centre.
3. Check the need for a mobile team.
4. Set up priorities (for hot beverages, etc.)
5. Determine special dietary needs and cultural food preferences.
6. Start a log (for food, equipment, etc.)
7. Check supplies and restock as necessary.
8. Contact food suppliers.
9. Ensure hygiene and sanitation guidelines are enforced.
10. Check safety and security measures in the food area.

11. Contact back-up staff (if necessary).
12. Prepare public information about:
    — meal hours
    — menus.

Continuing priorities

1. Brief the FS Chief.
2. Establish daily FS schedules.
3. Stay in contact with other Reception Centres.
4. Keep FS personnel abreast of all changes.

Closing

1. When the emergency is over, check the food service area to ensure everything is in order and refrigerators are empty.

Guidelines

1. A Food Service Log is Essential: A log facilitates smooth and effective FS operations. The log should include:
   — major management decisions;
   — daily summaries of meals served and problems encountered, and
   — any change in the numbers fed.

Use the log:

— to brief replacements or a superior;

— to keep track of borrowed, donated, and purchased equipment or supplies;

— to refer to earlier decisions, and

— to maintain continuity.

The Food Supervisor may appoint someone to maintain the log.

2. Daily Schedule: Draw up regular schedules for all FS activities.

Schedules

— make it easier to manage the Food Service;

— ensure essential tasks are done daily, and

— establish hours for meals and coffee breaks.

3. Administrative Services

Administrative procedures—the paperwork or "red tape" portion of a reception centre's operation are necessary and important. Initiate these procedures at the start of the EFS operation and continue them until disaster evacuees return home or are relocated. Basic administrative procedures involve:

— establishing and maintaining records related to food supplies, services, expenditures (if any), equipment (donated, borrowed, or purchased) and special problems (tag or mark all borrowed articles);

— setting up daily meals schedules, and

— filling out forms.

4. Daily Supply Report: Every day the Food Supervisor tells the FS Chief about additional supply needs. Supplies are co-ordinated by the FS Chief.

Role of the Public Health Inspector

Determining the scope of the emergency

The Public Health Inspector (PHI) can help determine the scope of the disaster and how it will affect the local population. The PHI can also help prevent serious disease outbreaks from food or water contamination during a disaster. Such problems can threaten health more than the disaster situation itself. The PHI, in conjunction with health and environmental laboratories, can monitor problems to determine health effects on the local population and propose remedial measures.

Monitoring would cover:

— the direct effects of a toxic spill or a similar disaster;

— the effects of secondary toxins released during a flood or a fire, and

— residual effects to food, water supplies, and local habitation.

Include the PHI in all discussions about emergency requirements, including building needs, water and food supplies, and waste disposal. The PHI monitors reconstruction efforts to ensure prevailing health standards are met.

Training Responsibility

The Food Service Chief trains or arranges for the training of FS staff. Training covers all aspects of the FS operation, as well as individual assignments. The FS training programme should cover :

— Community emergency planning

  — Explain the roles of municipal emergency response organisations (such as police, fire, health, and public works departments).

  — Explain the role of the Emergency Planning Co-ordinator.

— Emergency social services

  — Describe the four other Emergency Social Services.

— The FS

  — Purpose

  — Responsibilities

  — Organisation
- FS Resources Survey and Directory
  - Basic rationale
  - FS Resource Survey Records: how to complete them.
- FS Operational Guidelines
- FS at reception centres
- Emergency Food Management
  - Purpose of the reception centres
  - Role of the Food Supervisor
  - Reception centre services
  - Equipment and supply needs
  - Priority checklists and guidelines
- The FS Plan
  - Call-up procedures
  - Emergency priorities
  - Alternate provisions
  - Operating procedures
- The Log
  - Its purpose
  - How to complete a log form

The Chief of Emergency Food Service and EFS Supervisors should all receive basic training in Community Emergency Planning. Ideally, planning committee members should take courses offered by municipal, provincial and federal governments. The FS Chief or FS Supervisors determine the number of workers an FS needs. Recruit and train only key workers prior to an emergency. Recruit and train kitchen helpers, servers, dishwashers and others who do not require special training when the need arises.

Food Service Planning

In order to respond promptly to the nutritional needs of evacuees, the FS must have a written plan that can be implemented in an organised and co-ordinated manner as soon as a disaster occurs. The FS Chief and the planning committee develop a written FS plan in consultation with such municipal departments as:

— engineering (re: maintaining emergency equipment);

— fire (re: safety of designated FS buildings);

— public health (re: safe water sources and food safety), and

— transportation (re: safe transport routes for required food).

Once written, the FS plan forms part of the ESS response plan, which in turn is part of the overall community emergency response plan. The FS plan should therefore be considered in conjunction with these plans.

The FS plan should be clear, concise, realistic and always up-to-date. It should be flexible enough to allow on-site staff to adjust the plan as situations change. As part of the planning process, FS planners should try to anticipate typical FS problems during an emergency, and develop various solutions to the problems.

A plan should provide the following information.

(a) *Name*: A name will distinguish the FS plan from other plans.

(b) *Statement of purpose*: This statement establishes the plan's objectives.

(c) *Organisational details*: Use appendices to amplify a basic statement about the organisational structure and alternate arrangements.

(d) *Implementation Procedures*: State who implements the FS plan, and under what circumstances.

(e) *Alerting Procedures*: State notification procedures, using appendices to provide such details as: a key person alerts primary staff, alternates and essential community groups. Primary staff use a fan-out system to notify other staff members. Community groups alert their own staff.

(f) *Resources*: Amplify a basic statement with appendices outlining specific resource requirements covering:

— *personnel*—provide names, addresses and telephone numbers of all trained FS workers, with job assignments. Remember that you might require back-up staff if initial response staff become exhausted;

— *FS resources*—provide addresses and telephone numbers for prospective reception centres and contact persons (with home numbers as well), and

— *supplies and equipment*—list necessary equipment and supplies, sources of same and contact names, addresses, and telephone numbers.

(g) *Training*: Amplify a basic statement with appendices explaining:

— who is responsible for the training programme;

— when and where training will take place, and

—who will conduct the training.

(h) *Testing the Plan*:

— testing responsibilities

— testing frequency.

(i) *Reviewing and Updating*: Provide reviewing methods and procedures for updating the plan.

Letter of Agreement

Negotiate written statements of agreement with

organisations that have agreed to provide personnel, facilities, food or beverages, and equipment for the FS.

Mutual aid agreements

Mutual aid agreements enable adjacent communities to provide prompt and effective assistance in an emergency. Local governments should approve the plans.

Testing the FS plan

Once you have developed your FS plan, trained workers and located equipment and supplies, test organisational and operational response procedures and evaluate performances. Simulated exercises are effective. Devise exercises which could incorporate:

— minimum food supplies,
— minimum staff,
— unforeseen problems (such as equipment breakdown),
— emergency-type meals,
— mass feeding, and
— an improvised feeding area.

The Director of ESS or the Chief of FS should co-ordinate the exercises. Exercises reveal a plan's strengths and weaknesses, enabling you to determine whether positions are adequately defined and whether the plan can meet its objectives. Evaluate exercise results with staff. Correct the plan as necessary.

An emergency plan is of no use, of course, if no one knows it exists. Advance distribution of the FS plan to relevant emergency response organisations and service groups is essential to ensure co-ordinated efforts in an emergency.

Planning the Food Service in Institutions

Department of Dietetics

The Department of Dietetics should incorporate a written plan in the overall hospital disaster plan. Remember the hospital plan is part of the overall municipal emergency plan.

When a disaster occurs you must:

— determine the nature of the emergency and try to estimate how long the emergency will last;
— establish emergency priorities;
— determine staffing needs;
— assign emergency duties to qualified staff;
— assign duties in order of priority;
— ensure supplies and facilities are available;
— open a snack-bar on a 24-hour basis;
— maintain sanitary and safety regulations;
— ensure back-up staff is available to maintain service continuity;
— keep track of activities and problems in a log;
— inform staff of schedule changes, and
— be flexible enough to adjust to changing circumstances.

Guidelines for evacuation and relocation planning

Relocation

Hospital or institutional staff should be familiar with proposed relocation sites. The Department of Dietetics requires adequate advance information about a facility to plan an effective food service at the new site. Be certain a proposed site can meet your needs, and keep your emergency plan up-to-date.

Follow these steps:

— identify the relocation site;

— determine available space and make note of the physical layout, public utilities and available equipment;

— determine:
  - — food transportation methods
  - — service methods
  - — elevator and lift availability;

— identify:
  - — electrical outlet locations
  - — traffic flow
  - — exits and entrances
  - — dishwashing area
  - — garbage disposal area
  - — snack bar area;

— attempt to solve problems caused by:
  - — a loss of facilities
  - — damage to facilities
  - — an increase in the number of persons requiring food (residents, staff, patients, volunteers
  - — a lack of trained personnel for specific tasks
  - — staff fatigue
  - — a loss of institutional supplies
  - — the physical isolation of the institution
  - — picket lines, and
  - — attempt to restore interrupted services involving:
  - — transportation

— the delivery of supplies

— public utilities (water, electricity).

Relocation

When an FS is relocated to another institution, staff members normally join the staff of the receiving institution and are under the authority of the receiving institution's directors. Establish clear, mutuallyagreeable lines of authority in the planning stage. To carry out a smooth relocation, give staff specific evacuation assignments. Steps to follow.

— Select food.

— Assemble and pack food supplies.

— Deliver supplies to new location.

— Locate storage area.

— Determine priorities and ensure smooth operation of food service.

Negotiate in advance the use of schools, arenas, warehouses, churches or community halls for emergency relocation purposes. Food service facilities will vary according to the type and size of building selected. Typical examples include:

— buildings with facilities suited to both food production and meal service;

— buildings with limited public facilities which require slight modification or some additional equipment, and

— buildings with no cooking facilities but sufficient serving space, so food can be prepared elsewhere and brought in.

Improvise food service facilities, if necessary, in the new location. You will need to pay particular attention to:

— the physical layout,
— equipment and supplies,
— staffing and job assignments,
— operational procedures,
— sanitation (facilities and utensils), and
— support from municipal emergency services.

If meals are served outside, post signs clearly indicating the location of the food reception area.

Other planning guidelines

Expansion

Expansion increases the service capability of an institution. The food service department must be prepared to:

— feed more people, including
  — casualties, other institutional residents
  — relatives and friends of casualties
  — volunteers and workers; and
— provide an adequate and simple meal.

Progressive expansion

The progressive expansion plan must be flexible since it is used to plan the Emergency Food Service.

Maximum expansion

To run an EFS efficiently, consider the following points.

— Physical Facilities
  — Use existing facilities and staff, where possible.
— Menus
  — Discontinue selective menus;
  — set up emergency menus;

- — determine the number of meals required;
- — open 24-hour snack bar. (Use vending machines if necessary);
- — prepare a food priority list, and
- — alert suppliers.

— Staff

- — Consider additional staff needs;
- — plan to use key staff who may accompany evacuees arriving from another institution;
- — determine lines of authority;
- — line up qualified volunteers, and
- — plan assignments for supervised volunteers (Regular staff provide supervision).

Supplies and Equipment

Take supplies at other institutions into consideration when arranging supplies and equipment.

Food

— Assess the adequacy of average food supplies for emergency purposes.

— Arrange emergency food deliveries if needed (in conjunction with the institution's purchasing department).

— Consider stocking emergency-type foods. If you already have emergency-type foods, decide whether to rotate and/or enlarge the stock.

Dishes and cutlery

— Maintain enough disposable dishes and cutlery for meals for a few days.

Meal Service

For better meal service, speed and efficiency, follow these suggestions.

Tray service

— Use self-serve lineups, to avoid confusion.
— Use disposable dishes and cutlery.
— Plan an alternate method of food distribution.

Staffing

— Distribute food in the conventional manner and switch to self-service if needed.
— Open a 24-hour snack bar.
— Install vending machines, if necessary.

Modified siets

— Establish priorities for modified diets.
— Adapt these diets to the main menu.
— Develop a simple identification and distribution system.

Infant formula preparation

— Use regular methods to prepare infant formula.
— Use infant formulas, but continue to prepare therapeutic milk.

Community assistance

— Keep a continually updated list of institutions and agencies capable of providing special services or equipment.

— Arrange support from these organisations when the need arises.

Isolation

Each institution should have its own emergency plan to cover service disruptions caused by severe storms, floods, strikes, civil disturbances, or a national emergency such as nuclear fallout. The emergency plan should contain information about:

— additional sources of safe drinking water;

— water rationing and distribution;

— menus adapted to rationed food and water situations, or where cooking, refrigeration, and freezing facilities are lacking;

— food supply priorities;

— emergency supplies;

— the need for proper sanitation practices and safety regulations.

Co-ordinate the Emergency Food Service plan with the master plan.

Nutrition and Stress

Disasters have a profound effect on the eating habits of evacuees and emergency workers. Emergency Food Service provisioners must be aware of potential problems. The intense stress of emergency or disaster situations often causes people to forget to eat. Some will have more appetite than others. Pay particular attention to those who say there isn't time to eat, or who say they are not hungry.

Healthy individuals handle stressful situations best. A number of factors influence an individual's reaction, including:

— the type of stress,

— the intensity of the stress,

— the frequency of stressful situations, and

— the duration of stressful situations.

Tension, fear, and emotional upset can cause swallowing difficulties, loss of appetite or increased appetite, nausea, vomiting, hyperacidity, gas, bloating, diarrhoea, or constipation. Conflict produces similar emotional responses.

Stress can affect bodily functions to the point of provoking illness. Symptoms of stress include:

— stomach aches

— back pain

— ulcers.

Stress may also contribute to heart disease and cancer. Stress-related eating habits vary from individual to individual and are often under-evaluated or neglected. Consider the effects of stress when selecting food for evacuees and workers.

Menus should provide:

— light, easily digested food;

— non-stimulating drinks (fruit juices, water, lemonade, bouillon);

— light desserts, fruits, milk-based desserts, cookies, and

— high-energy snacks (plain granola bars, cheese, fresh fruits and vegetables).

Avoid spicy or extremely fatty foods such as pizza, french fries, smoked meat, and hot dogs.

Schedule regular meals and snacks. Provide snacks and beverages for workers at the rescue site. Be on the lookout for individuals who react to stress by not eating.

Feeding Workers

During a disaster, workers must receive adequate amounts of food. Long hours of work add additional stress. Guard against extreme fatigue by considering the following points:

Stress

Stress creates a degree of tension in workers. They may forget about the need to eat, especially if:

— their immediate tasks are urgent and enormous,

— the emergency is overwhelming, or

— sights, sounds, and smells are distressing.

Responsibilities rescue squad supervisors must:

— allow sufficient time for workers to eat,

— serve meals away from the disaster area,

— serve easily-digestible meals, and

— avoid heavy meals.

Rescue workers must:

— drink lots of fluids, especially when working in hot conditions;

— eat four to five times a day, in small amounts;

— eat a variety of nutritious food;

— develop a buddy system with a co-worker and remind each other to take breaks and to eat;

— eat regularly, whether hungry or not, and

— avoid drinking stimulating beverages such as coffee, tea, and caffeinated soft drinks.

Generally, serious fatigue begins after working four to six hours into most responses. If the use of caffeinated beverages could be delayed for at least four hours, personnel would gain the best physiological benefit from them.

Nutritious snacks are especially essential if the disaster continues for any length of time. In particular:

— encourage workers to drink 1 to 2 L (40 to 78 oz.) of water per day;

— provide juices or hot beverages, and

— replace doughnuts with fruit and nutritious snacks such as muffins, dry fruits, nuts, and granola bars.

If the disaster occurs when the temperature is high (34°C or 90°F), workers should drink a lot of fluids including mineral water and ready-made bouillon, to avoid dehydration. Salt may also be needed. Pay particular attention to the type of food served to workers performing the difficult task of extracting bodies from a crashed plane or the remains of a fire. Do not serve:

— chicken legs

— meat with bones

— spaghetti

— meat with burnt skin or skin that peels off easily and could bring back memories of recent rescue work.

To reduce the effects of stress, workers and evacuees should:

— eat at regular intervals,

— eat a variety of foods,

— eat several small meals if appetites are poor, and

— remember the need for additional nutrients.

Remember

— Disasters place extra demands on the body.

— Disasters disturb eating habits.

— Disaster workers require nutritious food.

Food Service in an Emergency Hospital

An emergency hospital is a prepackaged mobile unit equipped to handle 200 patients when it is set up in a suitable building such as a high school. Two shifts require about 260 workers. Mobile hospitals do not have kitchen facilities, so ESS and Emergency Health Services may ask the Food Service to fulfill the hospital's food requirements. Identify potential sites for emergency hospitals for the Food Service in advance, to ensure rapid response in an emergency. An emergency hospital is streamlined to essentials (minimum food service). Administrators should:

— improvise a kitchen;

— establish a serving area for staff and patients, and equip it with disposable dishes and cutlery, and

— when feasible, use pre-cooked meals.

Food requirements

Three general types of food would satisfy most patients and staff members in an emergency hospital:

— *Clear liquid diet*: juice, bouillon, consommé, sweetened tea or coffee.

— *Soft diet*: cream soup is the most suitable choice for the intermediate diet (between liquid and full diets). Foods must be easily digestible.

— *Regular diet*: a simple diet adapted to prevailing emergency conditions and kitchen facilities.

Nine FS employees are needed to provide meals for 460 people (staff and patients). They include:

— a supervisor

— a cook

— two to three assistant cooks

— four helpers.

Advanced Treatment Centre (ATC)

The ATC provides early life-saving care to the seriously injured. It also allocates the injured to available treatment facilities. Limited food is available at Advanced Treatment Centres. Hot beverages and cookies (survival cookies or granola bars) are essential so staff can maintain energy levels.

Mobile Feeding Unit (MFU)

In times of disaster, food does more than relieve hunger and sustain life. A properly timed hot beverage or a hot meal is essential to maintain the morale of evacuees. An MFU provides food for evacuees and workers when regular feeding facilities are temporarily not available. The MFU is equipped as a self-contained emergency feeding unit (exclusive of fuel and food). Use it to prepare and serve the following:

— one-dish meals, such as canned stews,

— meals in retort pouches,

— freeze-dried foods,

— hot beverages, and

— canned or dehydrated soup.

The MFU includes equipment and supplies for:

— purifying and carrying water,

— starting fires,

— opening cans,

— preparing, cooking, serving, and eating food, and

— cleaning, sanitising, and garbage disposal.

Heating and cooking equipment consists of a "Soyer" cooker with three large pots. Sufficient disposable eating utensils are included for several hours of operation.

Soyer Boilers

The "Soyer boiler" has a 45 litre (10 gallon) "working" capacity; its all-metal construction is suitable for boiling water, hot beverages, or stews. To avoid damaging Soyer Boiler and pots, observe the following precautions.

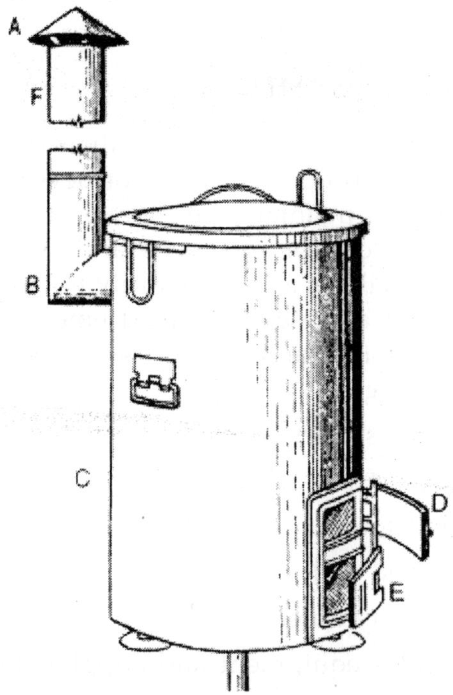

A – Cowl B – Elbow section C – Outer casing D – Firebox door E – Ashpit door F – Length of chimney Figure 1.

(1) New, tinned surfaces of the inner pots may be covered with protective grease. This grease is not harmful, but it should be removed before the pots are used. Use hot soapy water and rinse with hot water.

(2) Keep the inner pot at least one-third full of liquid when the unit is in use. If the pot boils dry, it will burn out.

(3) Maintain a low, steady fire under the pot. This requires frequent additions of a small amount of fuel.

(4) Pot damage will occur if the fire is built up too high, and if flames are allowed to rise above the level of food.

(5) Do not extinguish the fire with water as water causes rust and distortion.

Rake embers onto the ground, or allow the fire to burn out. In the latter case, either remove the pot or be sure that it is a least one-third full. Soyer boilers should be placed on a hard, level surface. If they have to be placed on tarmac, concrete or grass, a good layer of sand beneath each boiler will protect the ground from the heat of the fire. Ideally, piped water and drainage should be available nearby. Remove obstructions near boilers which could impede air flow. Fireboxes should face into the wind.

Bibliography

Angelo, Rocco M., *An Introduction to Hospitality Today*, Orlando: Educational Institute, American Hotel & Motel Association, 1998.

Astroff, Milton T., *Convention Sales and Services*, Cranbury: Waterbury Press, 1998.

Axtell, Roger E., *The Do's and Taboos of Hosting International Visitors*, New York: Wiley, 1990.

Baucom, Alfred H., *Hospitality Design for the Graying Generation: Meeting the Needs of a Growing Market*, New York: Wiley, 1996.

Boella, Michael John, *Principles of Hospitality Law*, London: Cassell, 1999.

Brown, Douglas Robert, *The Restaurant Managers Handbook: How to Set Up, Operate, and Manage a Financially Successful Restaurant*, Lauderhill, Atlantic Pub., 1991.

Buckner, Robert W., *Site Selection: New Advancements in Methods and Technology*, New York: Lebhar-Friedman Books, 1998.

Casado, Matt A., *Food and Beverage Service Manual*, New York: Wiley, 1994.

Chmelynski, Carol Ann Caprione, *Opportunities in Food Service Careers*, Lincolnwood: VGM Career Horizons, 2000.

Cichy, Ronald F., *Managing Service in Food and Beverage Operations*, Lansing: Educational Institute of the American Hotel and Motel Association, 1998.

Ellis, Raymond C., *Security and Loss Prevention Management*, East Lansing: Educational Institute of the American Hotel & Motel Association, 1995.

Emery, William H., *The Chef's Guide to Practical Restaurant Cookery*, New York: Van Nostrand Reinhold, 1988.

Gardner, Liese, *The Art of Event Design*, Malibu: Miramar Communications, 1997.

Katsigris, Costas, *Design and Equipment for Restaurants and Foodservice: A Management View*, New York: Wiley, 1999.

Katz, Jeff B., *Restaurant Planning, Design, and Construction: A Survival Manual for Owners, Operators, and Developers*, New York: John Wiley, 1997.

Kazarian, Edward A., *Foodservice Facilities Planning*, New York: Van Nostrand Reinhold, 1989.

Kim, Il-Sun Yang, *Inventory Control Systems in Foodservice Organizations: Programmed Study Guide*, Ames: Iowa State University Press, 1992.

Mills, Irving J. *Tabletop Presentations: A Guide for the Foodservice Professional*, New York: Van Nostrand Reinhold, 1989.

INDEX